Images from the Heart

What is a city but the human heart made physical...

—William R. Johnson
From the poem "Long Body of America,"
a section of which, set in Cleveland's Flats,
was published in *Denver Quarterly*, Summer 1993

Images from the Heart

A Bicentennial Celebration
of Cleveland and Its People

Cleveland Bicentennial Commission
Cleveland, Ohio
Publisher

Diana Tittle
Editor
and Project Manager

Eugene Pawlowski
Designer

Emerson Press
Morse Graphic Art Supply Company

Alling and Cory   American Greetings Corporation   The Bonfoey Company
Forest City Bookbindery (a division of the Chilcote Company)
KSK Color Lab Inc.   S. D. Warren Company

Dodd Camera & Video   KD Color Lab
Midtown Imaging   TSI Typesetting Service Inc.
Cosponsors

Copyright © 1995 by the Cleveland Bicentennial Commission

All rights reserved. No part of this publication may be reproduced or transmitted in any form, or by any means, electronic or mechanical, including photocopying, recording, or any information storage and retrieval system, without permission in writing from the publisher.

Photographs are covered by claims to copyright noted in the sections entitled Juried Contributors and "Community Shoot" Contributors on pages 136-141.

ISBN 0-9646667-0-7 (hardcover)
ISBN 0-9646667-1-5 (softcover)
ISBN 0-9646667-2-3 (limited edition)

Library of Congress Catalog Card Number: 95-69954

Additional copies may be ordered by writing or telephoning:

Cleveland Bicentennial Commission
1121 Terminal Tower
Cleveland, Ohio 44113
(216) 687-1996
Individuals and organizations

Octavia Press
12127 Sperry Road
Chesterland, Ohio 44026
(216) 729-3252
Trade

Photo supplies Dodd Camera & Video
Photofinishing KD Color Lab Midtown Imaging
CD-ROM image scanning American Greetings Corporation
Canon color copies Morse Graphic Art Supply Company
Canon color laser prints TSI Typesetting Service Inc.
Copyediting Kathleen Mills
Type Bitstream Fry's Baskerville (1764) and ITC Tiepolo (1987)
Text paper 100 lb. Lustro Dull (hardcover and limited edition)
          100 lb. Warren Dull (softcover)
Paper manufacturer S. D. Warren Company
Paper distributor Alling and Cory
Lithography Emerson Press, Cleveland, Ohio
Binderies Forest City Bookbindery (hardcover)
         B & B Bindery Inc. (softcover)
         Esper Bindery (limited edition)

Foreword

Every Clevelander has a mental map of the city that may differ radically from official cartography. For some the city's boundaries are the corner grocery and the neighborhood church. The mental maps of others incorporate locations as distant from the city's geographical limits as Cedar Point and Blossom Music Center. Favorite places loom large in one's conception of the geography of the city. For you, Gateway, rather than Public Square, may be the center of Cleveland. For me, it's University Circle.

To expect a single photography book, even one designated as the official commemorative publication of the Cleveland Bicentennial Commission, to capture the quintessential Cleveland—that treasured terrain common to the mental maps of all its citizens—is to ask the impossible. Instead, in searching for the best way to represent the Bicentennial spirit in paper and ink, the Cleveland Bicentennial Commission decided to invite a group of talented photographers to share *their* personal visions of the people and activities that make our town special in a proposed coffeetable book. Decidedly not a paint-by-the-numbers portrait of life in this community, the photo essay that emerged from nine months of shooting throughout the city and its suburbs went mere comprehensiveness one better. The Bicentennial photographers returned with a view of Cleveland that is as fresh and provocative as it is deeply felt.

Thus, this book's title.

Images from the Heart seemed apt for another reason. The volume you are holding is truly a labor of love. Seizing the opportunity to express affection for their great, flawed city, dozens of Clevelanders donated their time, talents and financial support to *Images'* creation. You will find their names listed in the back. Space allows me to single out only a few for special mention here.

The volunteers included the members of the Cleveland Bicentennial Commission's standing communications committee, who conceived the idea of commissioning a contemporary photodocumentary portrait of Cleveland, and the forty-three photographers jury-selected as contributors to the book.

In keeping with Cleveland Mayor Michael R. White's recommendation that the Bicentennial celebration be inclusive of all segments of the community, the contributors hailed from throughout Greater Cleveland and ranged in occupation from college student to artist to retired firefighter. Each photographer devoted a period between August 1994 and April 1995 to shooting his or her "dream" assignment, and many spent weeks beyond that in the darkroom. They received only modest reimbursement of their expenses—and, now, heartiest thanks for a job well done!

Hired as the book's designer, Eugene Pawlowski, chairman of the graphic design/illustration department of the Cleveland Institute of Art, also gave unstintingly to the project. During the pre-design period he willingly assisted in such time-consuming preparations as attending quarterly conferences with the photographers, poring over their portfolios for those few existing images too irresistible to exclude and slogging through the first rough edit of the thousands of new images that were created. An ad hoc editorial committee also contributed immeasurably to the planning process. Its members met monthly during the project's initial stages to advise on a variety of publishing and organizational issues. One of the editorial advisory committee's many helpful suggestions resulted in the solicitation of photographs from members of the public. "Average" Clevelanders responded enthusiastically to the announcement of the "Community Shoot" program, submitting hundreds of interesting photographs for possible publication.

When it came time to recruit volunteer writers, the city's supposedly isolated literary community demonstrated the civic-mindedness for which Cleveland is justly famed. Thirty-two busy journalists, novelists, teachers and poets set aside their own work to accept a formidable challenge. Given extremely short deadlines and only a few lines of space each, they created a text that is as evocative and memorable as the images it accompanies.

Magic of another kind was performed by David Emerson, chief executive officer of the Emerson Companies, whose Emerson Press was *Images'* lithographer and its leading corporate cosponsor. Working diligently for almost a year prior to publication, Emerson put together a crack manufacturing team and a generous underwriting package that allowed the Cleveland Bicentennial Commission to publish a champagne edition on a beer budget. Emerson's personal commitment to the project put graphic excellence within reach.

Another of the book's munificent corporate cosponsors, Ken Morse, president of Morse Graphic Art Supply Company, should also take an extra bow. Morse helped to facilitate and foreshorten the lengthy design process by providing a seemingly endless supply of color copies of prints and transparencies, which were then scanned onto computer for use in rough layouts. Then, at a point at which others' generosity might have been exhausted, he elected to help underwrite an exhibition of selected images from the book at the Cleveland Center for Contemporary Art.

On display from October 13 through November 11, 1995, as part of the Center's imaginative celebration of Cleveland's 200th anniversary, *Images from the Heart* (the exhibition) was the satisfying culmination of perhaps the most ambitious book publishing project ever undertaken in Cleveland. I am proud to have been part of such a historic venture, whose many organizational challenges were made lighter by the good offices and humor of the Cleveland Bicentennial Commission's staff leaders, Dave Abbott and Ann Zoller.

—Diana Tittle
Editor and Project Manager

There it is, friend. That's the north coast of Middle America you're looking at. A river cut a chink into the forest here and men wedged in and took the trees and left a city. The city grew tough and made its living with sweat and smoke. The city was the nation's forge for a while and white-hot steel was beaten flat here by refugees from an old world who never saw home again. They brought grainy photographs of grandma standing in the wheat. They brought bridal dresses in tissue paper. They brought recipes and religions and they spoke unintelligible English camouflaged by the accents of a score of Europe's smaller kingdoms. So they learned to speak American from the newspapers and from the slang their kids brought home from school. They poured and hammered themselves into a mold they hoped was American. But they left their music alone.

We're a bit too far offshore to hear it. But it's there. Accordions and Gypsy violins and a klezmer band. Bazookas and mandolins and a polka band. Harmonicas and banjos from West Virginia. Saxophones and a blues guitar once played in the backroom of a "colored" store on a Saturday night in a nothing town in the apartheid South. They wrapped their hopes around a tune and carried the tune with them, the people who came to live here, and their songs blended and became part of the musical score of the city.

And the city itself sang. Railroads sang and rapid transit trains and trolleys screeching on overhead wires. The Shoreway bridge sang when you drove over it. Ore boats sang around Collision Bend and the Thriller sang with Laughing Sal at Euclid Beach. Merchants chanted at the West Side Market and priests chanted in neighborhood churches. Cantors sang in synagogues and on the front porches old people crooned tales of old countries that they had heard from their parents who had sung them to sleep with them. The song of this city called new immigrants and is calling them still. The finest musicians in the world come as pilgrims to the stage of Severance Hall and their polished instruments sing with the world's greatest orchestra. Rock musicians come here to be crowned the best of the breed. Ah, it is alive with music, our town.

So, in this book, a chorus of voices sings a song that is uniquely our song. It is a blend of "Happy Birthday" and "God Bless America" and "Take Me Out to the Ballgame" and other anthems and requiems of remembrance, scored for a staff that is drawn from the grid of our streets and tuned to the key signature of our neighborhoods. It is a song that is in your bones if this town is your town.

Listen.

Glacier-scoured rock holds a prehistoric memory of a blue day, perhaps 12,000 years ago, when a mile-thick wall of ice finally recedes. Floating debris, warm winds, scuttling water everywhere bring forth a new epoch, a new solemnity.

An old tale to come out of the Ohio Territory was that a squirrel could cover the width of the state moving from tree to tree without so much as scraping the ground. When one walks through the old-growth forest in the Metroparks, one gets a sense of how dark it must have been—an endless cycle of routine and sunless days. Imagine the first blows of the ax, the felling of the trees, the single figure of the frontiersman clapping his hands, reawakened, reinvigorated by the sacredness of light.

Big bluestem, Indian grass, dense blazing star. Rangers and volunteers at Brecksville Reservation gather seeds, hundreds of species. Through careful management—replanting, controlled fires—a prairie ecosystem slowly begins to remember itself.

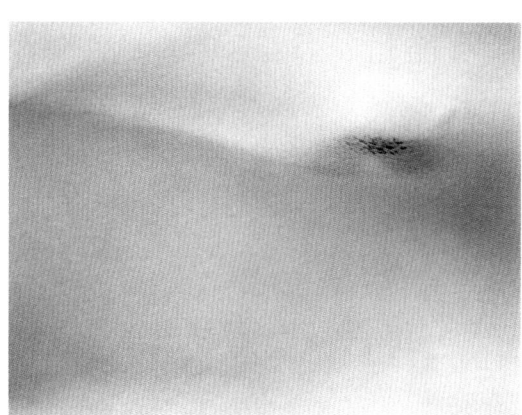

The Cuyahoga's headwaters seep from snow-covered glacial till near Burton.

Moundbuilder, early conveyor of goods, the solitary canoeist reminds us of a forgotten past.

Near remnants of canal beds, we hear the voices of the old drovers with their mule-pulled packets of corn, whiskey and wheat. The great shuck and pound of train wheels carried Cleveland to prominence as a mercantile center. Now millions of semis, tires slapping concrete joints, swarm around the warehouses. Yet between the interstates, beneath the great concrete abutments, one still feels the movement of the river.

The Cuyahoga stays its course past slag piles, old smelteries and rolling mills on its way toward the bright pleasure corridor of the Flats.

15.

One of the great hearths of industrial America, magisterial and decaying, Cleveland's Flats is a strange cathedral of solids, voids, cylinders and planes.

Stand on the west bank of the Cuyahoga River, looking east, and you'll get the big picture: a 3-D story of a frontier village that grew into a thriving

city of smokestacks and skyscrapers, fueled by ready access to a wealth of natural resources and the energy of men's and women's dreams.

"Tremont was where they came, from West Virginia and Eastern Europe, to be close to their work, in sight of it. They lived in houses built into the rising sides of the industrial valley like steps, their scraps of yards blooming with roses and hollyhocks and bounded with scrolled ironwork fences, on streets named for a never-realized vision of a university—Literary, Professor, College. Like thousands of other newcomers to the city, my parents lived there, unknown to each other—my father on Seymour, my mother on West 14th, fresh up from the country."
—Mary Grimm

Towering above the Ritz-Carlton, a still lake of white linen and murmuring silver, the Society Center is a glossy advertisement for the city's new service economy. Its product: a ceaseless flow of information, which records the fury of our days. Beneath nervous streets one can hear the cacophonic sound of a mechanical timepiece: the RTA rapid diligently keeping its appointed rounds.

Peel away the layers of Public Square and what do you have?
Public Square still.

Over the years they tried to change it, put a fence around it,
call it something different. They even try to beautify it. Like it
needs it. Ten acres of New England-style town commons,
buried under layers of solidified steel smoke and battered by
Lake Erie winds: a community's aspirations, anchored in reality.

It is where the city is divided east and west—but also its common ground. Though it was envisioned as a meeting place by early settlers, it's a traffic light, a bus stop or an ashtray to many. It has been visited by history, over the streets that crisscross it, on the tracks that run underneath, even on its sidewalks. President-elect Lincoln stopped here on his way to Washington—and on the somber trip that finally took him back home. When Charles Brush unveiled his arc lamp here in 1879, Public Square basked in the brilliance of his invention. And yet, it is no stranger to darker days.

Through it all, rising through the layers, the soul of the city is revealed in its Public Square. It shows the way, like Brush's lamp, or a courageous new leader. Flowerbeds and fountains, at the center of the urban core. It is the city's imagination, a collective vision of its people. It knows what is and wonders what could be.

Hello! At last count, 11,196 babies were born in the City of Cleveland during a twelve-month period. The spark inside these children is worthy of our most serious attention and respect.

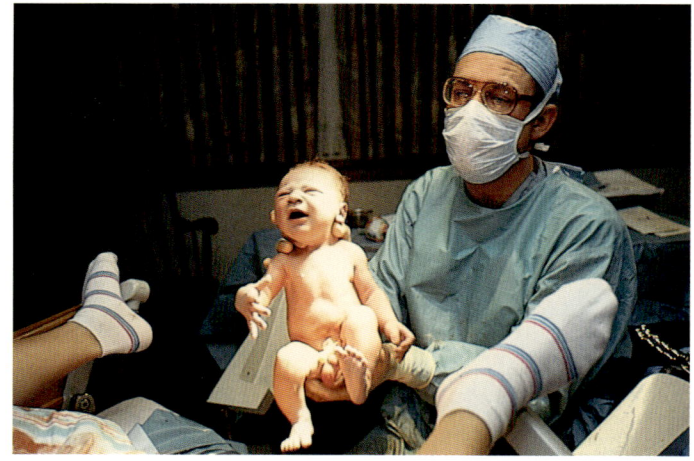

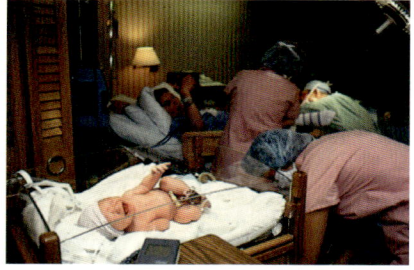

We know *where* we are—growing up in a Midwestern metropolis, a major-league town, the birthplace of rock and roll. Our parents are white-collar, blue-collar, pink-collar. Our friends are white, black, and brown, Irish, Italian, and Polish, Protestant, Jewish, and Catholic.

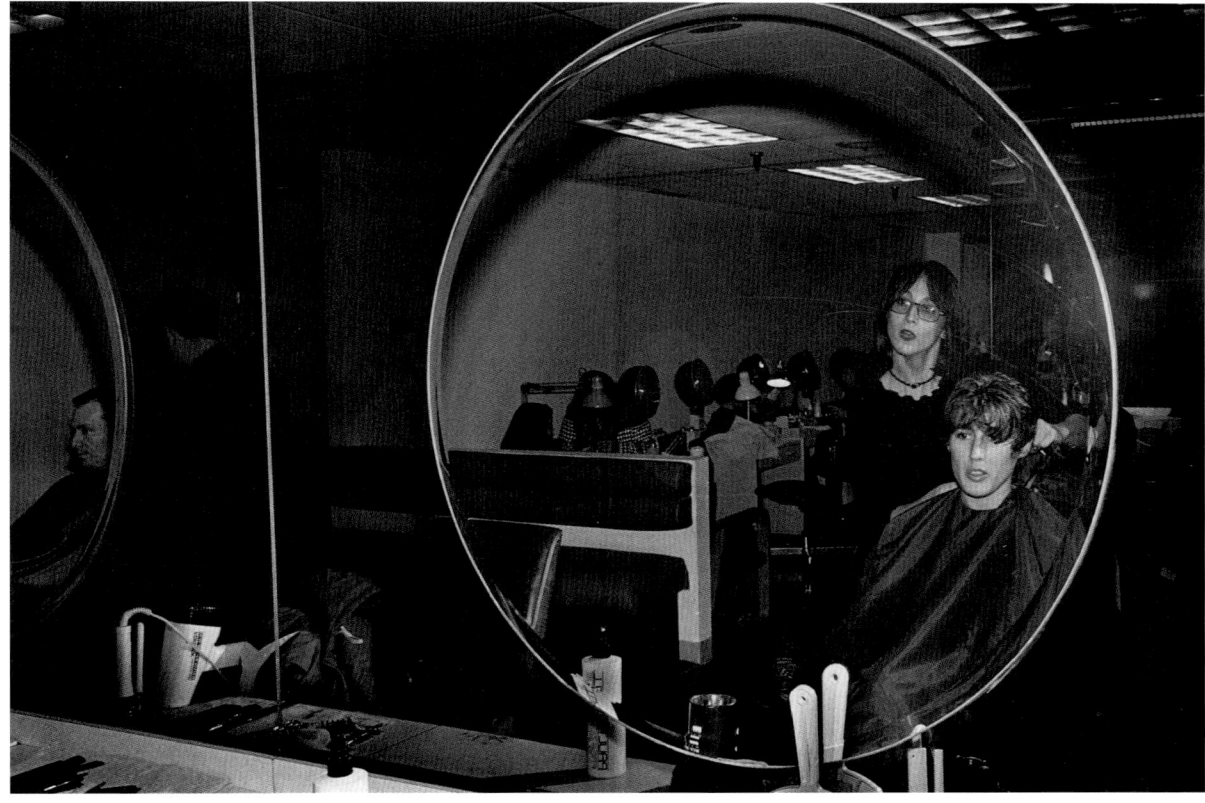

So let's try to figure out *who* we are. In between the routines of school and home, let's head for a place where all these people come together—where we can see and be seen, where we can improvise and experiment a little. Let's try on a different look, take in a new movie, pick a new CD. Who knows? Some of it just might fit into this identity we're putting together—this bicycle that each of us must build while we're riding it.

The dark women who crossed the Ohio River,
the dark women who knew definitely
movement as freedom, the dark
women who called the river, *blood*, and said,
Cleveland, as they might have whispered, *life*,

loved in that shameless way, deep down.
This they passed on and it holds as a keepsake.

More than fifty nationality groups call the city home. Clevelander Frances M. Longar refers to her ethnic background as Slovenian. Her parents came from Bevke, Yugoslavia.

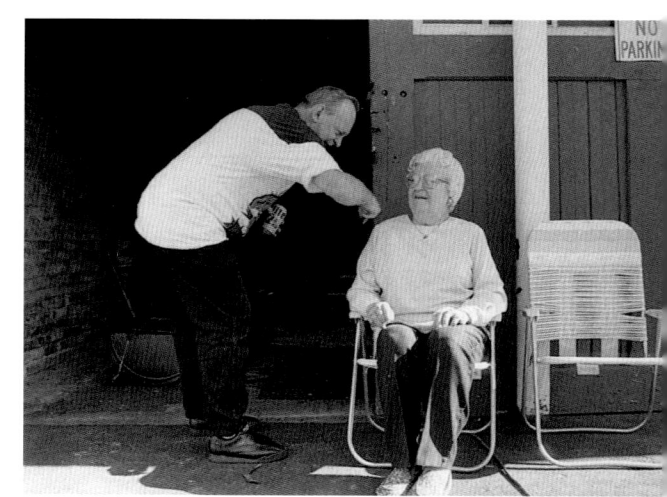

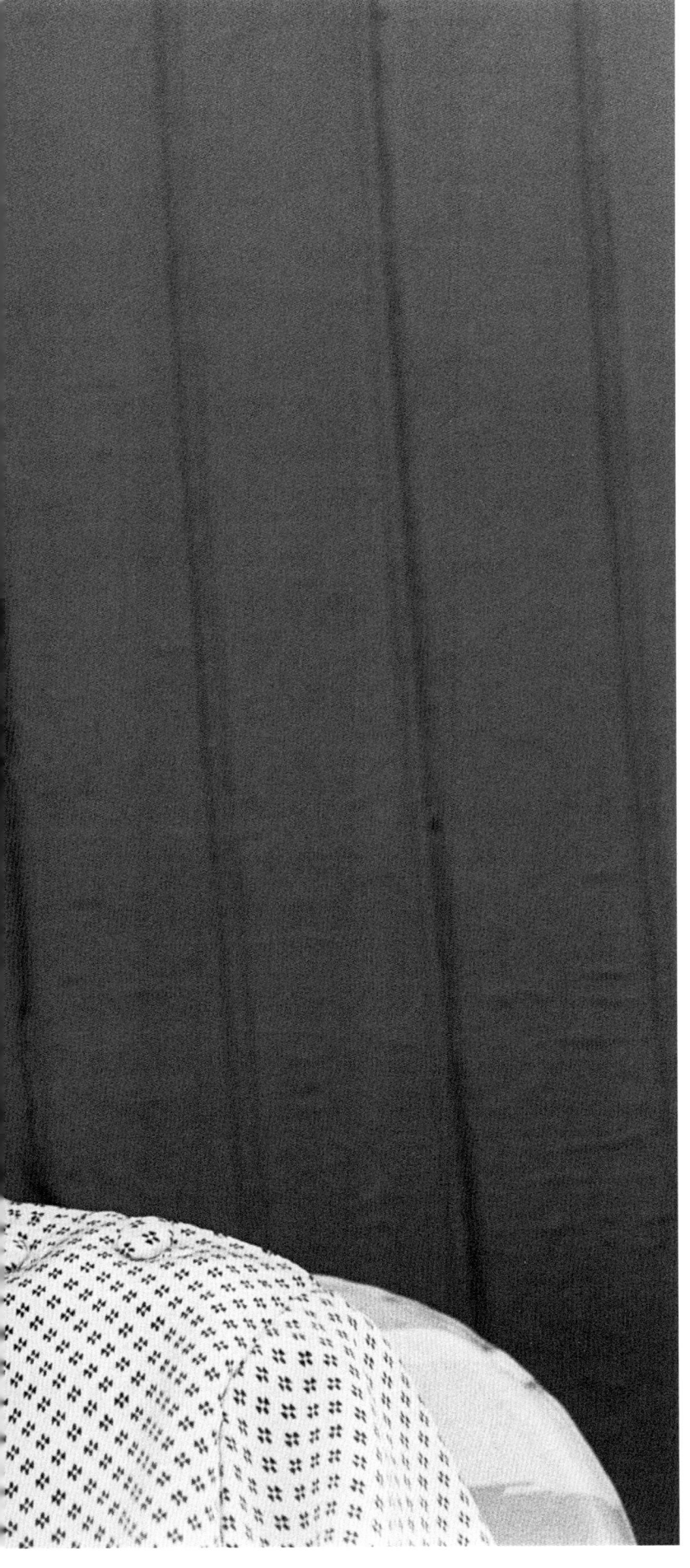

Mrs. Longar was born on Norwood Road near East 55th and St. Clair. Before the war she moved with her husband, Frank, into Cleveland's Kirkland neighborhood near East 40th and Superior, where she has lived ever since, the matriarch of a family of six children, twenty grandchildren and ten great-grandchildren.

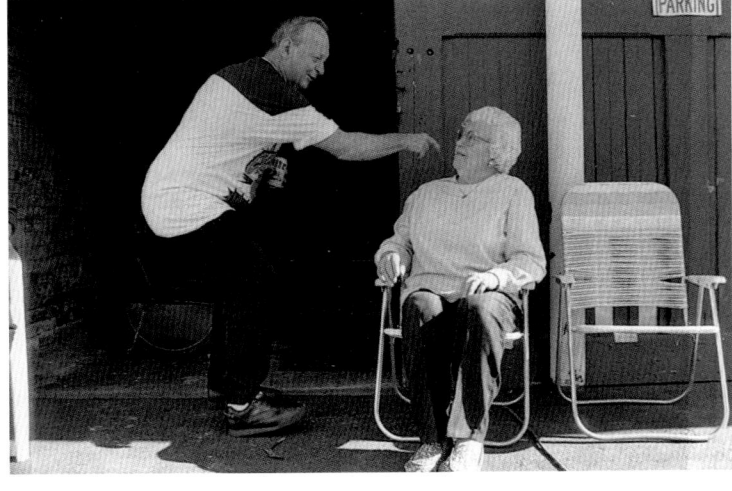

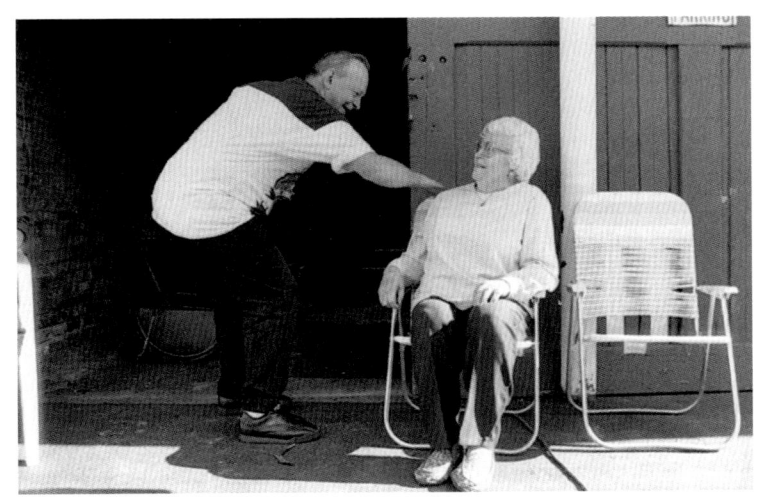

"When we moved into the neighborhood we had one family, Piorkowski, with fourteen children. Jones had eleven. Then on 40th Street Uroic had nine, Sallays had ten and we had six. We were all large families. The house was crowded. There was never a dull moment. It was a good life.

"In 1943, after we were married a few years, Frank came home from work one day and says, 'Well, you know, we're going into business.' I said, 'What do you mean?' He said, 'We got a place on 40th and St. Clair. It's a meat market.' I looked at him and…what the hell, he was boss of the family. Here we are fifty years later. I didn't realize it was that long."
—Frances Longar

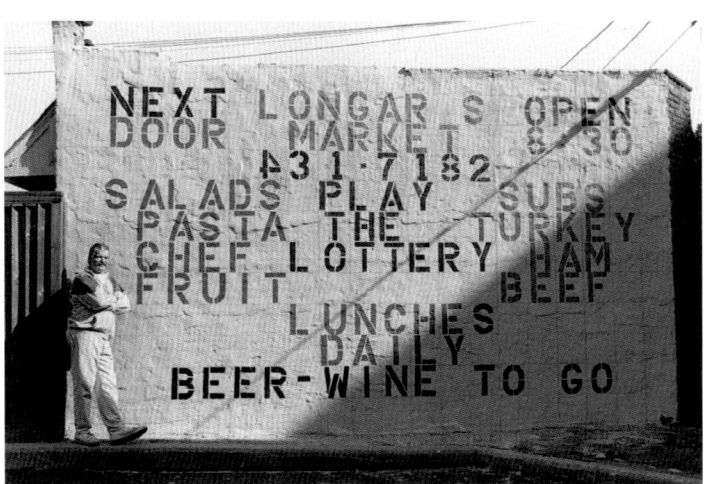

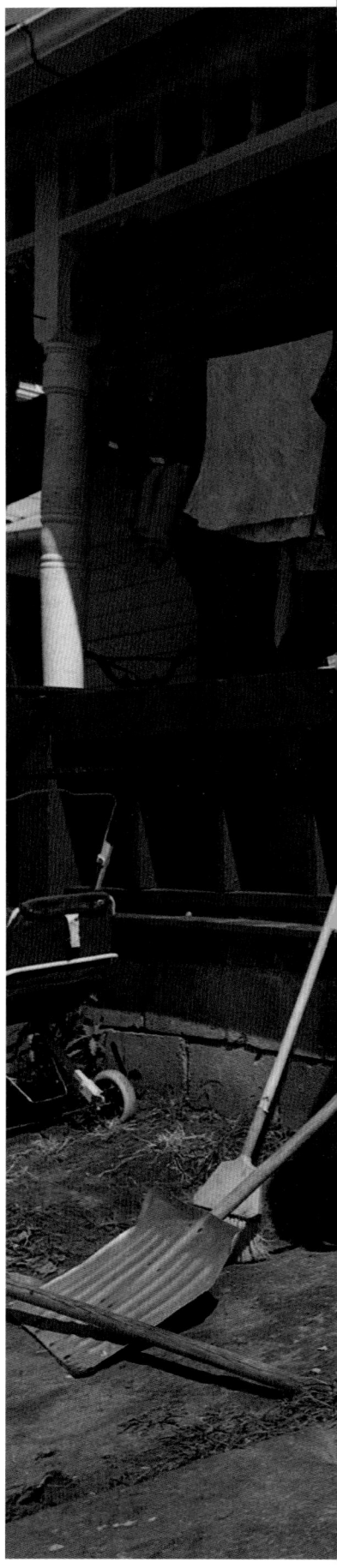

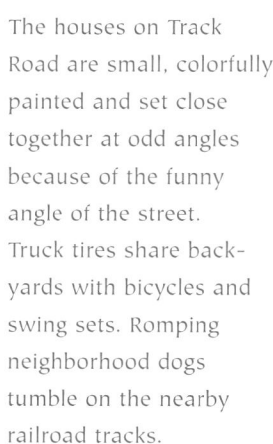

The houses on Track Road are small, colorfully painted and set close together at odd angles because of the funny angle of the street. Truck tires share backyards with bicycles and swing sets. Romping neighborhood dogs tumble on the nearby railroad tracks.

A huge black oil tank is parked on a rail spur scant feet from where muscular, solid men and women resting from their long, hard workdays sit on their porches to enjoy the smart breeze that snaps the clean laundry on the line. The open, flat-planed Slavic faces of parents and grandparents smile cautious welcome over the chain-link fences that make good neighbors.

The names on Track Road's mailboxes evoke the nations of Eastern Europe that tourists seldom visit. They also evoke America—the America that smelted the steel and loaded the trucks and laid the tracks and worked the railroad. Generations of sweat got them here, these children of immigrants who proudly fly the Stars and Stripes and wear patriotic tattoos, to this, their own small piece of Cleveland and the American Dream.

"The Number 6 bus that takes us out Euclid Avenue can be crowded even on a hot early summer afternoon—elderly ladies with ankles so big they must hurt, young girls trying to keep their babies quiet, businessmen loosening their ties and squeezing their eyes shut, a group of younger men crowded at the back and talking loud politics. A man in a winter coat gets on and announces he's the Fresh Prince of Euclid Avenue and he's looking for a butterfly woman to be his Queen, and the driver kicks him off and we look at one another knowingly.

"The old woman next to me fans herself and glances over at the book I'm reading, which is *Showplace of America: Cleveland's Euclid Avenue, 1850-1910*. We look at a picture of a horse-drawn trolley with 'East Cleveland R.R. Co.' painted on the side, traveling a rail along what looks like countryside with streams and groves of trees and stately manors and such.

"The old lady shakes her head and then she pulls the 'Stop Requested' cord, and the bus glides to the curb and the doors open like an exhaled breath."
—Dan Chaon

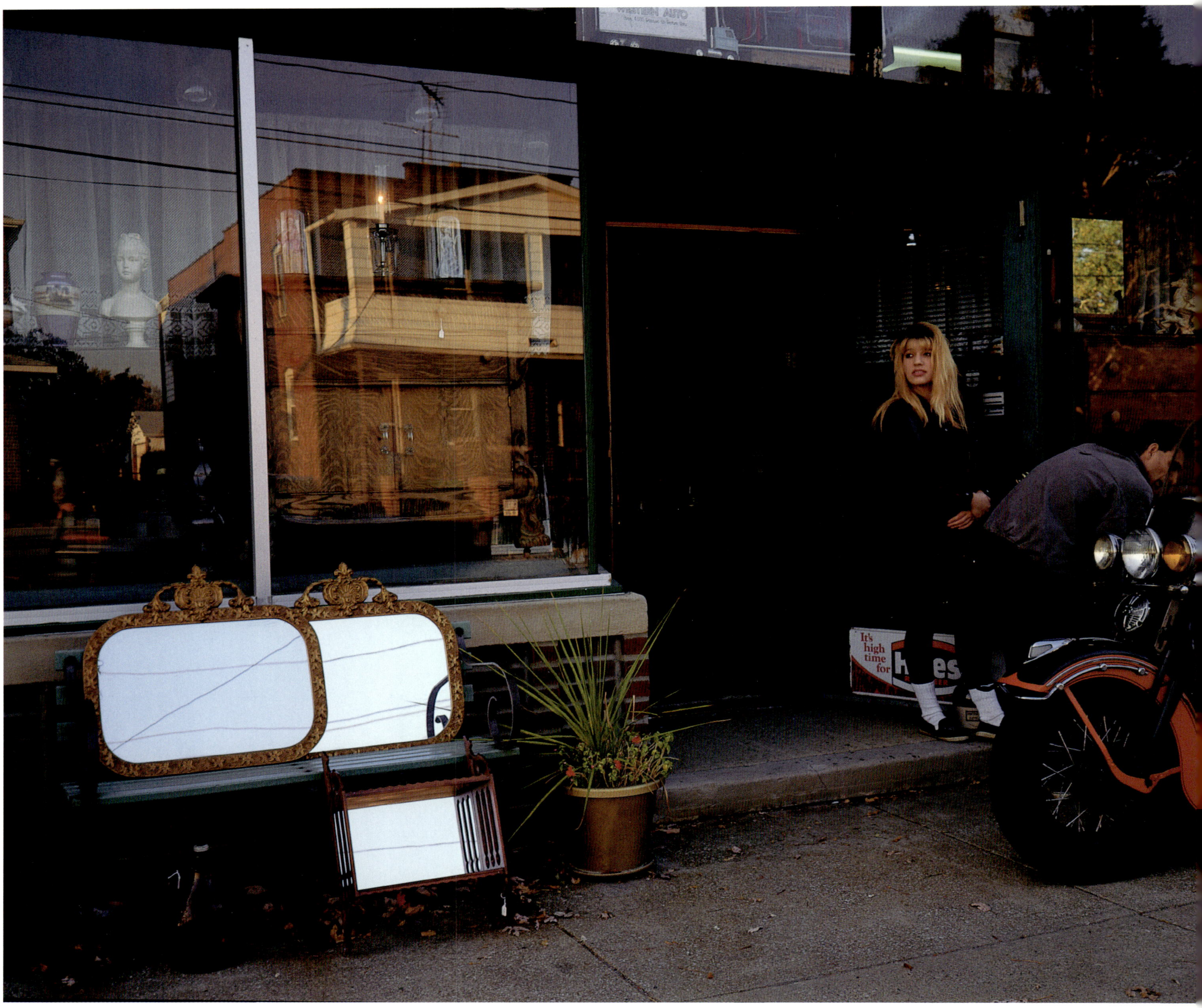
It's high time for

IN HONOR OF

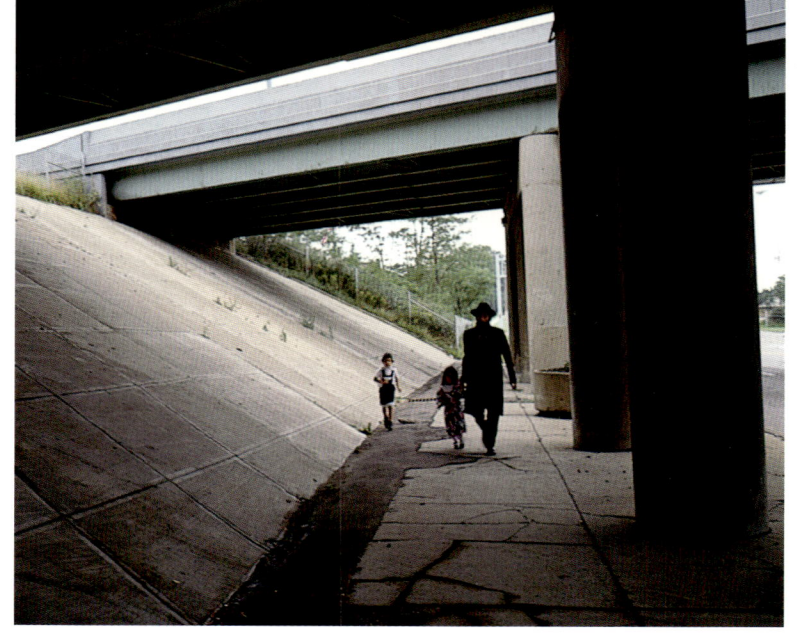

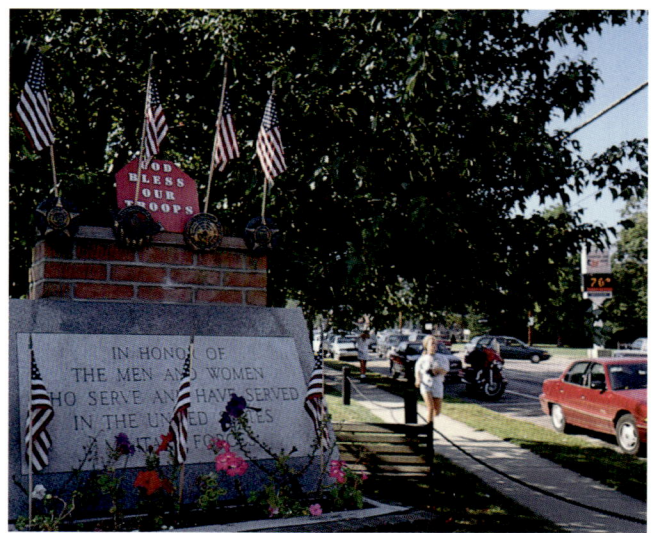

Out in the heart of the state, a "small town" is a cluster of buildings and houses surrounded by countryside. Here, the small town is a state of mind. Wickliffe melts into Willowick and Willoughby, and the casual traveler might not notice that one town has merged into the next. This is not to say that the boundaries aren't significant.

The town knows itself as an entity, stakes a claim to independence. Here is the old main street with its row of storefronts, the city park, the summer fair and farmers' market, the occasional parade with the high school band making its slightly discordant way down a street that once led "out of town."

Eventually, of course, the string of interconnected towns does end. It begins to break off into peninsulas and archipelagos and islands farther and farther apart, and the edge of Cleveland disappears like a coastline, a shore in the distance.

A remarkable vision of suburban living became a reality in this city after the turn of the century.

Before the Great Depression could slow the process, turrets and gables, mock battlements and Tudor timbers, manicured lawns and lush gardens would combine to evoke "country house" grandeur in the lakefront suburbs of Cleveland's West Side and its majestic "heights" to the east.

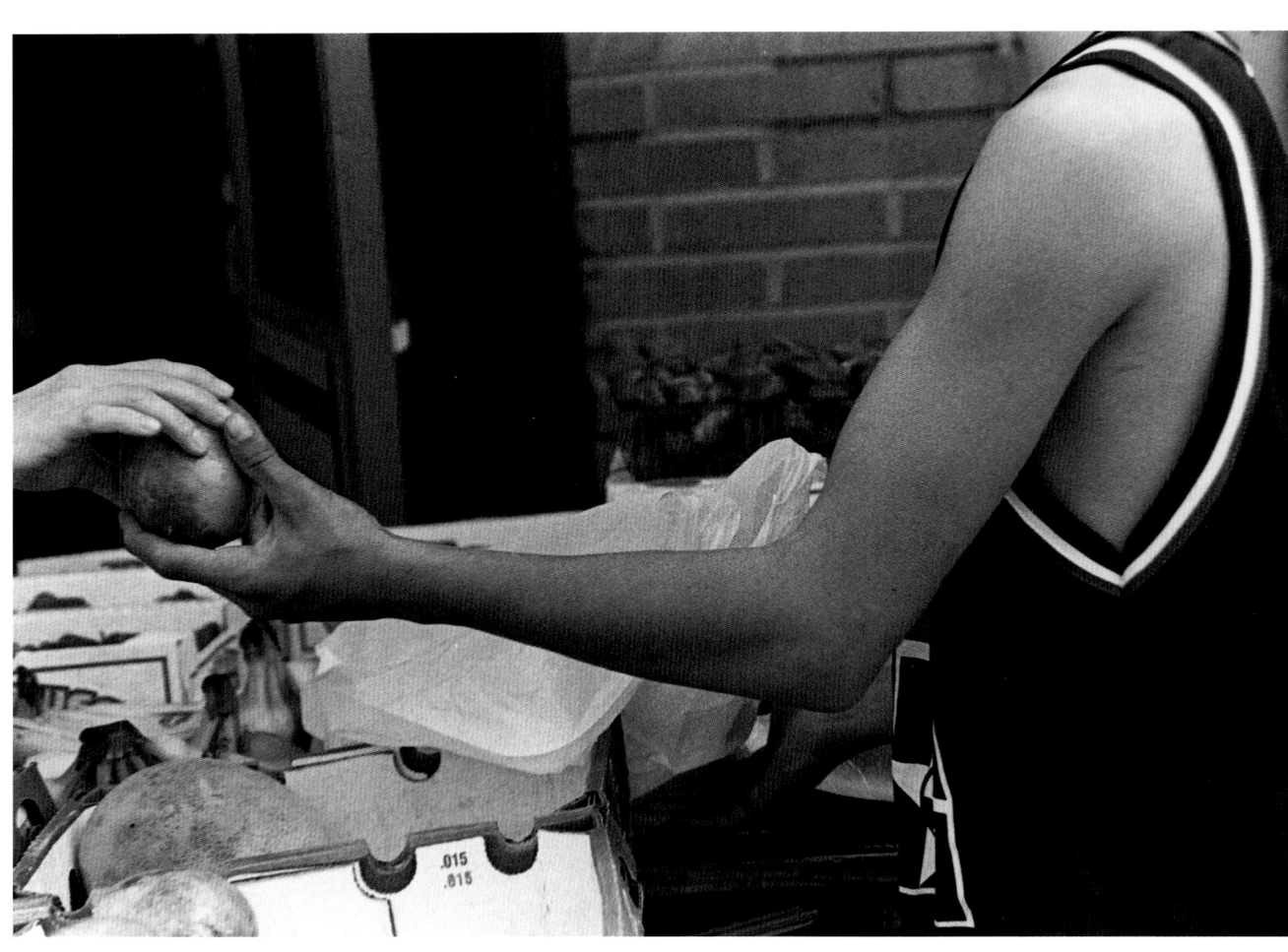

Few places in town bustle with the shoulder-rubbing activity of the West Side Market on a Saturday morning.

The air is alive with the aroma of cheese and sausages. Glass cases are arrayed with fresh pork and pierogi, short ribs and shanks, hams and hens, scrod and squid. Mouths water at the sight of tortes and babkas. Above it all floats the constant rise and fall of seller and buyer haggling and laughing over food.

Coventry Road has the Ara-freaka. University Circle attracts the Ara-geeka. Shaker Square boasts the Ara-chica.

Arabica. Coffeehouse of equal parts caffeine and atmosphere. Drink your cold café mocha outside with some wacked Deadhead fella. Listen to the bongo-drum-playing-batik-wearing-dreadlock-shaking man. Share a light with a loner on her last smoke. Catch some hacky sack. Read a book. Better yet, write a book. (Or, just say you're writing a book.)

Music and talk. Poetry and Russian tea biscuits. This is Arabica. And as the clock nears "close," and people drift away, perhaps then you'll find a seat.

There is something besides its public places and people that defines a city. Something not so obvious. Something that stays, even when the people are gone, and something that lingers, despite the changing skyline. That ineffable aspect of Cleveland reveals itself between the hours of 3 a.m. and dawn.

Much of the region's natural beauty derives from an abundance of parklands, each with a distinctive personality. The civic impulse from which they all sprang was articulated by Cleveland's first park commissioners, who sought to create "a harmonious development of sylvan beauty to which all are welcome, rich and poor alike, where all may find rest and inspiration and pleasure."

Clevelanders are fascinated by the infinitely changing moods of Lake Erie. We sit on the boulder-strewn breakwalls with our feet dangling over the edge,

and in the space of a daydream we witness the lake whipped into a frenzy by a passing storm. It's our wilderness. Every day we take a long drink.

"Lake Erie? We don't say 'Lake Erie.' We just say 'the lake.'

"It's like my father's crazy brother, my uncle. He's always been there. I can't remember a time when he wasn't there. Sometimes I go weeks without seeing him, sometimes longer, but I know he's there.

"He's a bad drunk, you know? Every so often he gets crazy, violent, even. Sometimes people get hurt. But when that happens, it's no surprise. It's just him.

"So sometimes we're scared and with good reason. And sometimes we're embarrassed. But we come back. When I was growing up I never had more fun than with him. Most of the time. And I'll tell you: When I look back, I only see the good times. Plus he's family.

"That's the lake."
—John Tidyman

From across the Great Lakes and foreign ports as far away as Turkey, Russia and Japan, some one thousand cargo ships and freighters converge on the Port of Cleveland each year, delivering upwards of fifteen million tons of commodities vital to manufacturers and consumers throughout the region.

Coal.
Consumer goods.
Grain.
Iron ore.
Limestone.
Sand.
Steel.
Stone.
Two hundred trucks a day are needed to disseminate incoming shipments of these materials.

An unusual icon of a proud industrial history is the family of four Hulett unloaders poised at the water's edge.

Mechanical giants like these once dotted the shores of Lake Erie and the banks of the Cuyahoga River, emptying, in short order, Superior iron ore from the holds of freighters.

Now those at the C&P Ore Dock are the last survivors. They seem to turn a cold shoulder to the pile of ore nipping at their heels, rust-red pellets deposited by self-unloading boats that made the Huletts obsolete.

In his 1966 book, *The Cuyahoga*, William Donohue Ellis likened the Hulett unloaders to "genial monsters," adding that "they smack their steel lips with a clatter that shakes the whole of Whisky Island." Today the mechanics, the oilers, the Hulett operators are gone. The machine shop is silent. The dinosaurs sleep under the watchful eye of a lone sentry.

Seventy-six Cleveland firefighters
have fallen in the line of duty.
Who mourns these forgotten heroes?

It's always been a Hot Metal town, pal. Always and forever. Just puddles of liquid fire, at first. Then the Civil War changed everything. Soon it was Hot Metal on a grand scale, all up and down the twisty river. Open hearth, blast furnace, Bessemer converter. Great bubbling cauldrons of the precious brew. We're talking Big Steel, fella. Acre after acre, and the sky as red as a cherry. Hanna-boats and Mather-boats, bringing in ore to feed the hungry mills. Whaddya mean, "What mills?" Otis. Corrigan-McKinney. Jones & Laughlin. Mr. Cyrus Eaton called his baby "Republic." Then LTV set the sky aglow.

But hold on. Who's going to work this Hot Metal? Earn a living? Raise a family? "I'm your man" sang a chorus of voices, from New World and Old. They came. They worked. They raised their families. And something else, too. Because, truth be told, a Hot Metal town can build itself. Hell, a Hot Metal town can build a country. Railroads, skyscrapers, bridges, bobby pins. Ore boats, lunch buckets, airplanes, pickup trucks. Tanks, when you need them. And little red wagons, too. That's steel, bud. Just tell us how much you need; we'll take care of the rest.

"What's not to like about downtown Cleveland? Yeah, it gets a little noisy, a little crowded, and traffic on East 9th before a Browns game can be murder. But hey! If I wanted to spend my life watching TV out in the suburbs, I could.

"No telling when there's going to be a parade on Euclid Avenue. Can't think of anything I rather do than hang out on Public Square. Great place to study hemlines. One time I shared a park bench downtown with a guy who claimed to have God's mailing address. There's usually people strutting around downtown who think they know how to run the world. Well, maybe they do. I'm willing to listen. There are worse ways to spend a lunch hour. Downtown's my neighborhood. I work here. I live here. Gotta love it!"
—Buster Jackson

Maybe it's because of the ironic sense of humor that seems built into the psyche of industrial towns that have seen it all. For whatever reason, kitsch is big business here.

An old Chatty Cathy doll, a scratched copy of the soundtrack to *Exodus*, a ticket stub from the '54 Series, a Monkees lunchbox—unearthing one of these treasures on Lorain or Larchmere elicits from us a delighted "Ay caramba! I haven't seen one of those in years!"

They said it would never last—this noise blasting out of the basements and bars of blue-collar America with all the subtlety of a jackhammer or a punch press.

But, after forty years, rock's still as hot as a blast furnace, charged up as a transformer, powerful as a bulldozer, wild as a runaway train.

A hall of fame for its heroes? Who would build it? *We* would, and we have! We got the job, we found the site. We worked overtime to raise the money and build this cathedral—the First Church of Rock and Roll.

Three chords and a cloud of dust, baby!
Let's plug it in and crank it up.

Like an order of crazy, wage-weary monks
They file into Moe's after third shift.
Stan, Jimmy and Bobby Z.,
Hydraulic yawl still in their ears.
Beer for breakfast,
Chasing grace-cups of Early Times.
The heavenly voices of Smokey, Tammy and Muddy
Fill the air.
Two hours between foremen, sleep and family.
Benediction.

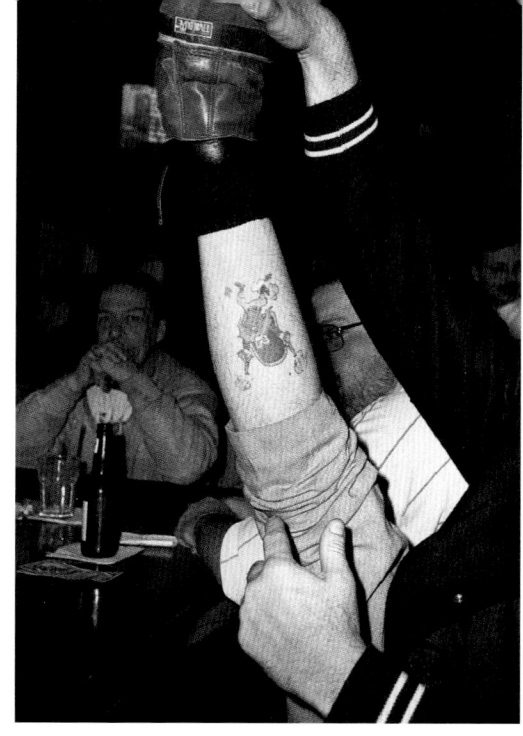

Where do they go after midnite? after the oasis?

What traces do they leave behind?

A joyful noise—

The food of love—

A little R-E-S-P-E-C-T.

Jazz makes the living look easy…

...makes it seem like summertime all year long.

76.

Wheee! In the frantic-happy movements of all those who partake of a fair's manufactured joys— the slides, spinning rides, the giants on stilts, the games and their prizes— you can see the ghost gestures of an earlier time, when people came together at the annual county fair to celebrate their shared community.

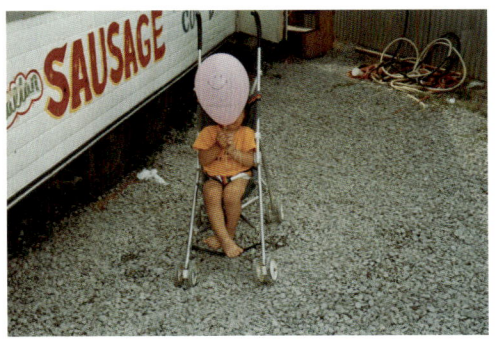

All too often Cleveland youth claim their childhoods from an inheritance of urban woes, but these guys aren't thinking of any of that. Just check them out, practicing their moves at a homemade basketball hoop, performing gravity-defying flips, playing baseball at League Park.

Cleveland kids have been inventing their own fun ever since the offspring of Lorenzo and Rebecca Carter frolicked in their parents' log cabin at the city's first social dance on July 4, 1801.

Those Connecticut Yankees had the right idea: Work hard, play hard. It's like that still in the city they created. Because toil is the price you pay for a little fun. And even the fun can be demanding. Want to win this game? Plan your moves with the cunning of a Clausewitz.

Want an equal share of the goodies? Divvy them up one by one, so all can see.

Want to soar like an eagle? Sweat your way through the legs and arms and heaving chests that block you from the net.

Put in the effort, use everything you have—work at it. When nothing comes easy, the rewards are that much sweeter.

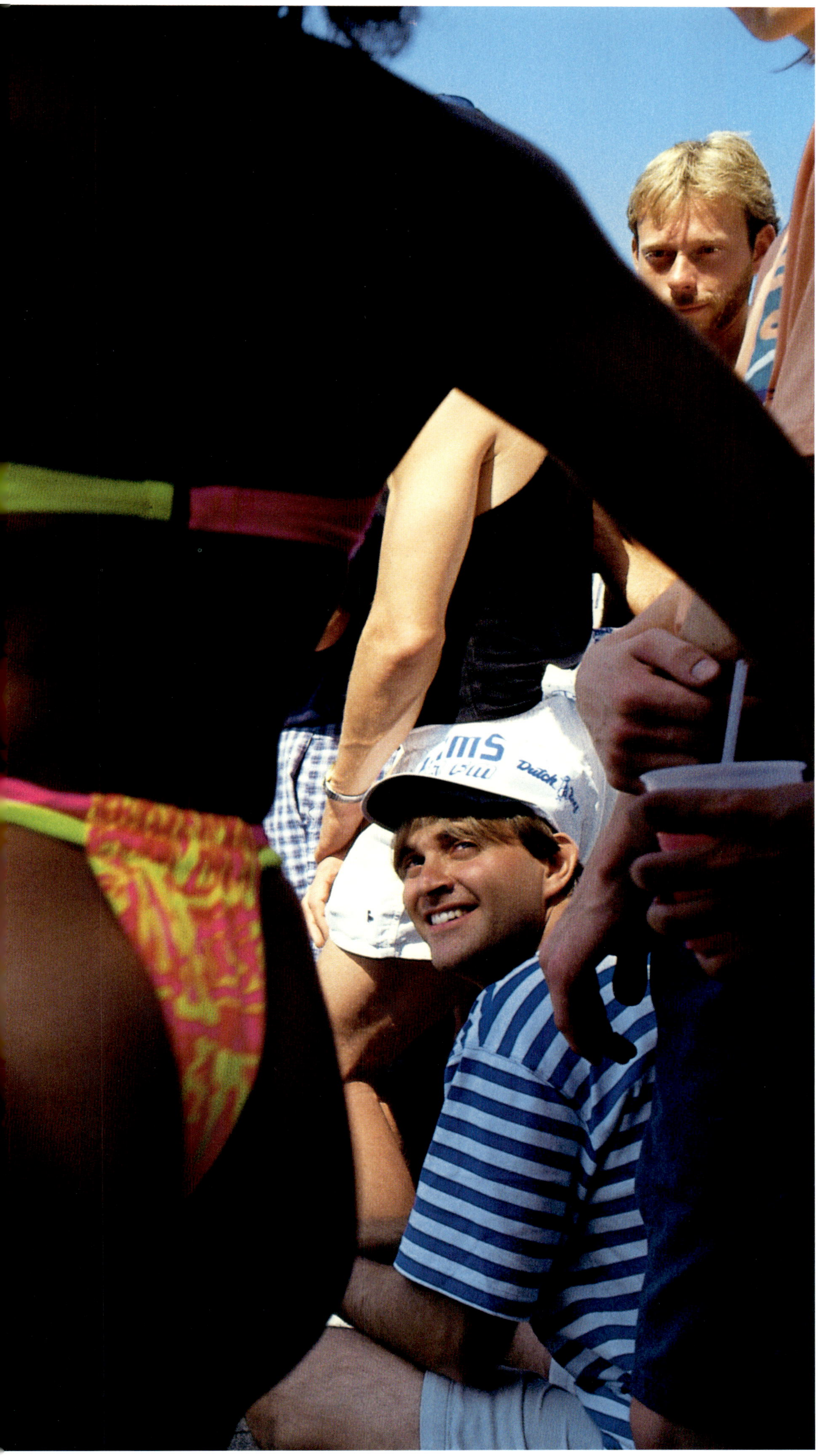

Ogling the opposite sex can be one of life's harmless pleasures. But nobody visits the Flats for innocent fun. Not in the valley of the party. Even when practiced in the bright sun this is still a night game. The Flats is where Clevelanders go to play it.

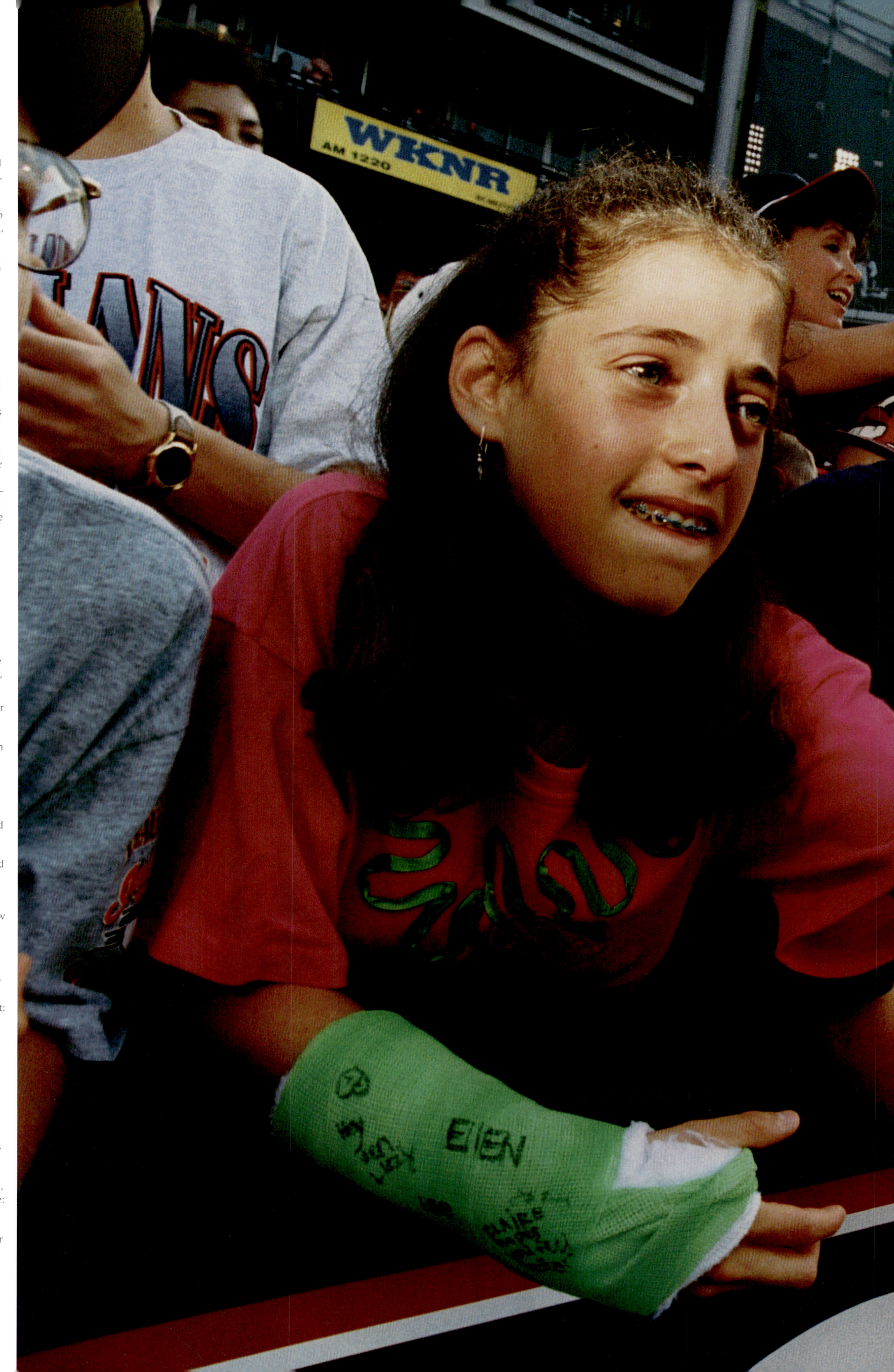

"Two months after I moved to Cleveland, I cast my vote for Gateway. I couldn't see what was not to like: a new ballpark, in a part of the city where nothing was, paid for by a tax on stuff you shouldn't do anyway. The next year, when I first saw the plans for that ballpark, it took my breath away. I couldn't understand why no one else seemed giddy. In January of 1992, ground was broken, but the city greeted the news with fatalism. *Looks good, but things have looked good before.* A year later, a Gateway official told me that everywhere she went, people came up to her and told her Gateway was never going to happen. Have you been downtown lately? she'd say. The girders are in place; the cement is poured. And people would shake their heads and say, *We'll see.*

"I spent the summer of 1993 in Mexico. Coming back, my airplane swooped in east of Cleveland in a wide arc over sunlit Lake Erie, then banked south and came in, low, over the city. I could see the Terminal Tower, and the Cuyahoga River, and all those handsome bridges. We came in lower still, and there it was: the new ballpark, almost finished, gleaming in the summer sun. And my heart knocked against my ribs, and my spirit soared, and I thought: *Home. I am home.*

"A year later, I sat in the left-field stands. Opening Day at Jacobs Field. On the pitcher's mound was the President of the United States. Around me was this lovely green thing, better than you'd have dared to dream, and all these people: these Clevelanders. We Clevelanders."
—Mark Winegardner

The twenty-member congregation of Puerto Rican Protestants at La Iglesia Cristiana makes up in devotion for what it lacks in size.

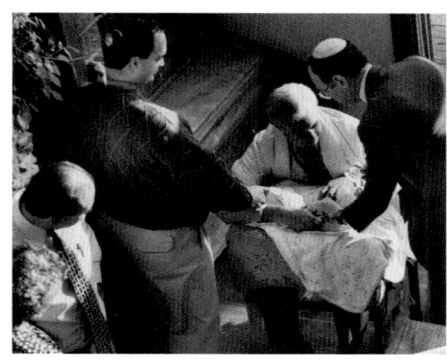
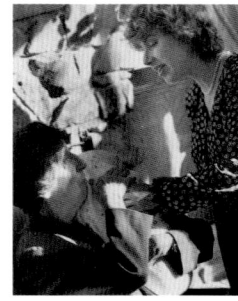

The Temple-Tifereth Israel is home to the second oldest Jewish congregation in Cleveland. The *Brith* is the ceremonial welcoming of the newest member of the Jewish community. Do you sense a continuum here?

With more than twenty-five thousand Muslims living in Greater Cleveland, Ramadan has become a prominent religious observance. On the last day of this month of fasting, some of the faithful gather for the inaugural prayer service in their new place of worship, a $3.5 million mosque housing men's and women's prayer halls, a library, lecture hall and even a mortuary.

The gilded rotunda of the men's prayer hall was inspired by the classic Dome of the Rock in Jerusalem, while its airiness echoes the reverence for nature found in the graceful mosques of the Iberian Peninsula.

From meetinghouse plainness to Victorian Gothic splendor, Cleveland's sacred landmarks have weathered time to retain a symbolic place in the heart of changing neighborhoods. St. John's Episcopal, the oldest standing church in Cuyahoga County (below), survived a fire that destroyed the interior, a tornado that blew off part of the sanctuary wall and an earthquake that shook the foundations. St. Michael (left) went from a nationality parish for Roman Catholic Germans to a neighborhood church serving the needs of Puerto Rican and Mexican immigrants. Other magnificent church buildings were demolished after congregations fled to the suburbs and the grand structures became too expensive to maintain. The historic churches that have endured testify to the commitment of those who gave their leadership, money, labor and love to preserve these sanctified places that lift the spirit and speak to the soul.

More than thirteen hundred congregations were listed in the metropolitan Cleveland phone book at last count. These included 320 Baptist, Congregationalist, Methodist or Presbyterian churches and 157 Catholic, 98 Lutheran, 63 Pentecostal, 44 "nondenominational," 40 Church of God, 30 Jewish, 28 Eastern Orthodox, 23 Apostolic, 18 Jehovah's Witnesses, 17 Assembly of God, 14 Christian Scientist, 14 AME and AME Zion, and 7 Holiness congregations as well.
—From *The Encyclopedia of Cleveland History*

God is in the details of Cleveland's historic churches, and so is the identity of congregations past and present. At St. Patrick's, the nostalgia of Irish immigrants is expressed in shamrocks that decorate the soaring structure.

At St. Stephen's, painted statues have the fair complexion and golden plaits of the church's German founders, while at St. Adalbert (top) the skin of some Biblical figures was painted black when the former Bohemian parish became the first African-American Roman Catholic congregation in Cleveland. At Trinity Cathedral, a choir of carved angels sings praise in the Anglican tradition.

Although most architectural details are part of the original fabric of ecclesiastical buildings, the murals in the Marian Shrine at St. Vitus were recently added to commemorate World War II martyrs and refugees from Slovenia.

Always there remains the story
of the individual.

The name survives in the very stone
covering the body over,

as if memory must begin at the end.

Still the city remains. The street
continues. The bricks
from the old church appear
again in the new church.
Without warning the next century
lifts its lids and only
the weathered headstones
feel the force. The stone graves
give a little, breaking apart
until each reveals the lived through
lines in the palms of the dead.

The plaque says you're a Moses Cleaveland tree. A committee measured the diameter of your prodigious trunk (with a steel tape held chest high) and certified that you date from the time of surveyor Moses Cleaveland's first and only trip to the wilderness of the Western Reserve in 1796. You managed to survive two hundred years of European settlement, land speculation, agriculture, lumbering, commercialization, industrialization and suburbanization.

Against disease, drought, wind, lightning, insects, soil compaction, air pollution, a thousand small insults that weaken trees and eventually kill them, you stood stubborn. You rooted in this place and kept sowing your seeds. Two hundred years. A million seeds. A million hopes. Against all odds, you are going to regenerate the forest.

The Greek Orthodox monks who run St. Herman's House of Hospitality on Franklin Boulevard don't consider it a homeless shelter. St. Herman's, they say, is "a house of prayer," a monastery with twenty or thirty extra beds. A neighborhood man peeling potatoes in the kitchen says it is "a place for healing wounded spirits."

The homeless men who eat and sleep at St. Herman's do chores, such as cooking, washing dishes or preparing bags of food for others—and take the opportunity to read and reflect on the meaning of their lives and, as anyone must do who encounters this place, the meaning of community.

The families who originally settled the area around West 65th and Madison have moved on to places like Parma and Fairview Park. The front steps of the aging wood frame houses sag now with the tread of other laborers, and of men and women for whom there is no work.

But the churches they built—St. Patrick's, and the others that arose as that once teeming parish overflowed its pews (St. Malachi's on the river's bend, St. Colman's to the west and at least nine others)—still provide a place where neighbors can reach out to one another. And the news that "the people have nothing to eat" prompts a weekly miracle on the city's near West Side not much less impressive than the original one on that Biblical hillside.

On Monday nights, it happens at St. Malachi's, on Tuesdays it's St. Pat's, and so on, as more than two thousand hot meals are served, every week, to the homeless and the underfed of the neighborhood.

In the cheerful atmosphere that surrounds these meals, one realizes that human beings suffer many kinds of hunger.

Gardening is a healing art. To begin with, it heals the Earth.
For the gardener, toiling amid the beans and sweet corn heals the body,
while watching Nature's cycles heals the mind and soul.

Gardening can even heal a community's spirit,
as do Cleveland's shared neighborhood gardens,
which reclaim abandoned lots and return them to public benefit.

Clevelanders pioneered in the field of philanthropy, giving birth in the early years of the century to the concepts of federated fund-raising and the community foundation. Service to God, country and humankind remains a strong tradition here.

There is no social or cultural continuity—indeed, there is no city—without the schooling of children. And at the heart of the schooling enterprise are life-shaping transactions between adults and children: attention paid, skills imparted, complexities explained, competencies demonstrated, talents exercised and potentials stretched.

How ironic that the Dark Age of Europe was a Golden Age in Ireland. Scribes in monasteries meticulously copied and preserved the works of the church fathers, the Romans, the Greeks. In time the Irish monks took their learning to the Continent, where they became missionary-teachers.

How ironic that the Renaissance of Europe was a Dark Age in Ireland. Every effort was made to obliterate its language, culture and religion. Most of the Irish who emigrated to America in great, desperate waves in the nineteenth century could neither read nor write. But they brought what remained of their poetry, music, dance and storytelling.

Which is why the little step-dancer knows something of the *Book of Kells*. It is from that fabulous illuminated manuscript that her costume's intricate designs are derived.

Two hundred years ago during the period of Cleveland's founding, Beethoven began to compose music. Listening to the Cleveland Orchestra play those familiar old notes, imagining that the soaring rhythms fill the immensity of Severance Hall, we are reminded yet again of the timeless power of the creative spirit.

What is it about this town that attracts so many creative spirits? How to account for the surfeit of music, theater, dance and visual art? Is it the still-felt influence of the "old families" and the philanthropic traditions they put in place? Or a more visceral inspiration?...

…For those of us who have chosen Cleveland as our artistic home, there is an almost militant attachment to the no-frills reality of the place: the grayness, the grittiness, the unfashionableness. Few if any cultural trends are apt to be set aloft here anytime soon, but nowhere else are artists more engaged in the day-to-day life of a community. Taking their cue from Cleveland as a whole, they do their jobs without much fuss. An abundance of vigorous, resonant work gets created that way.

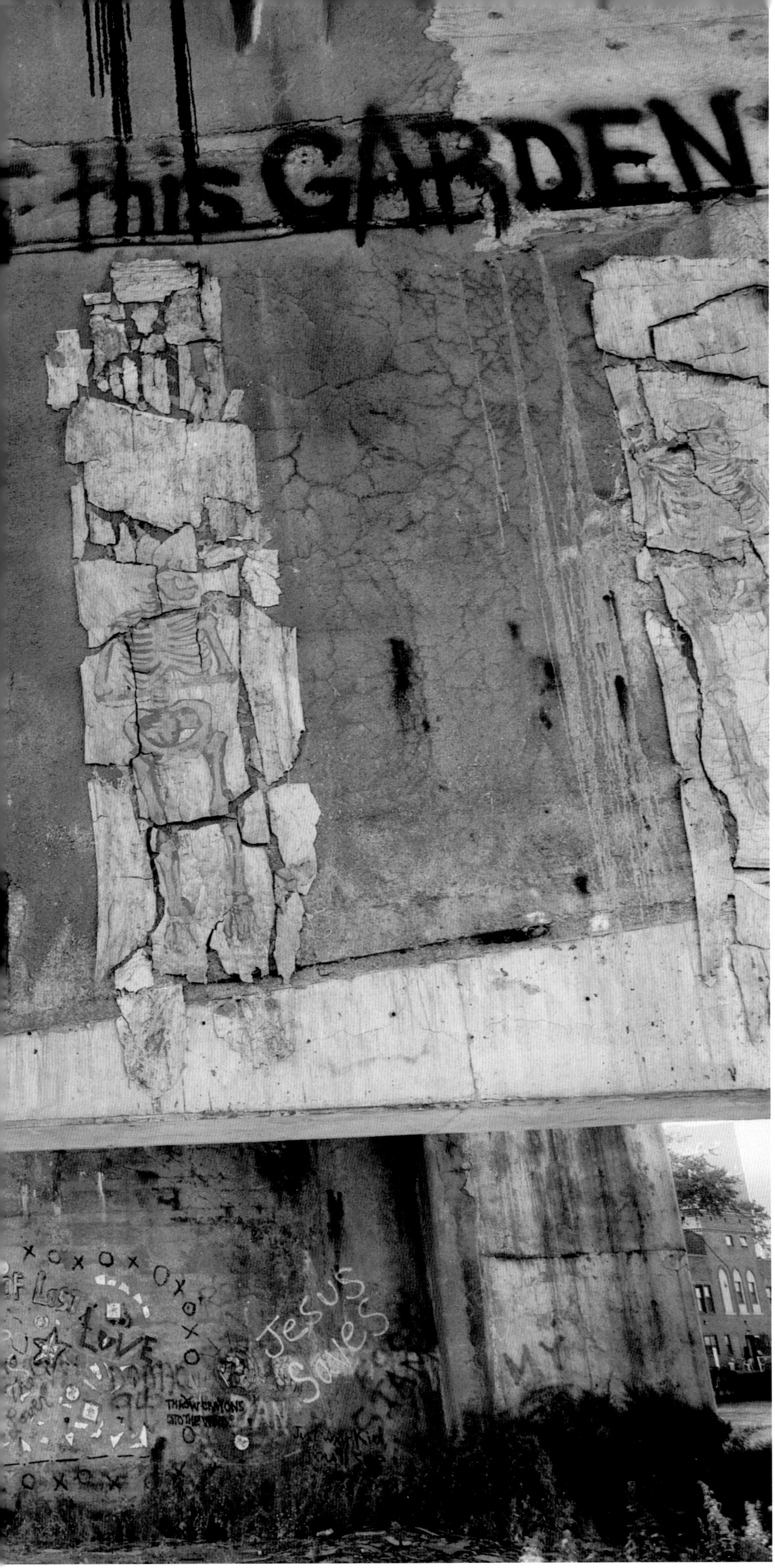
this GARDEN
LOVE
Jesus Saves

OF

LOVE
94

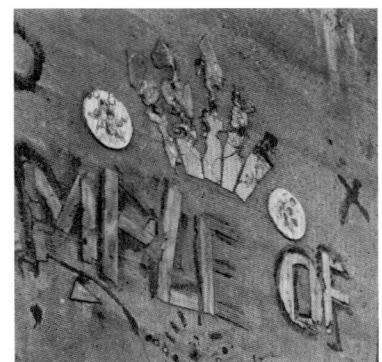

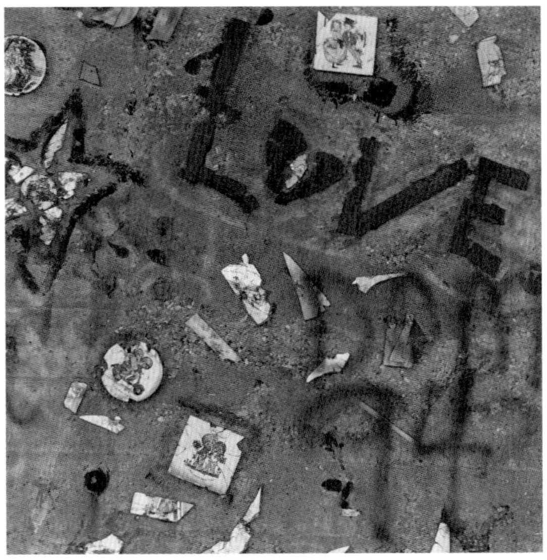

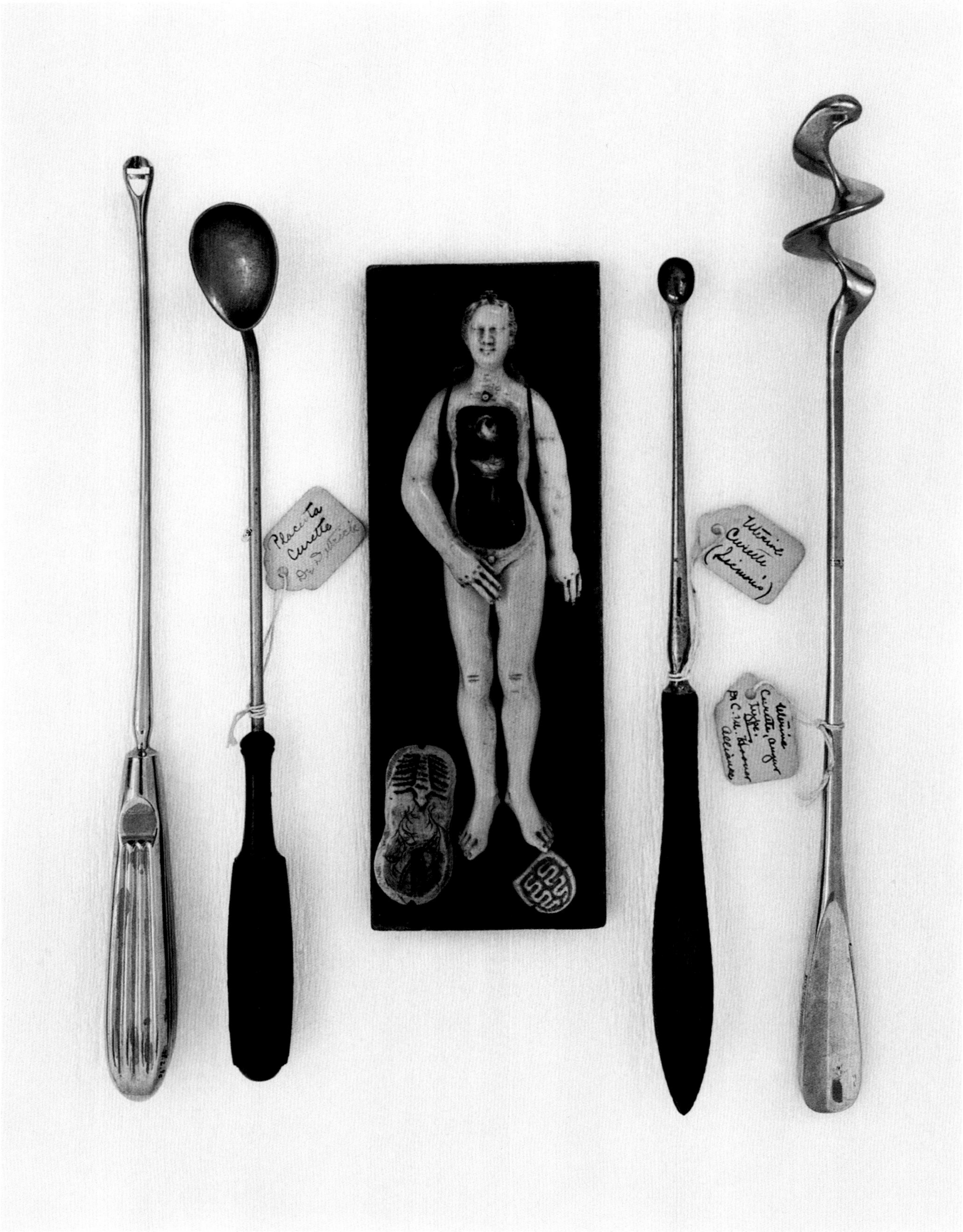

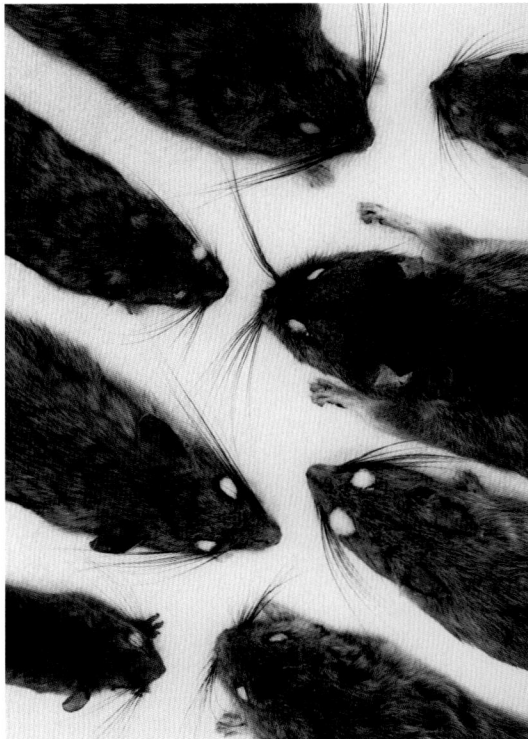

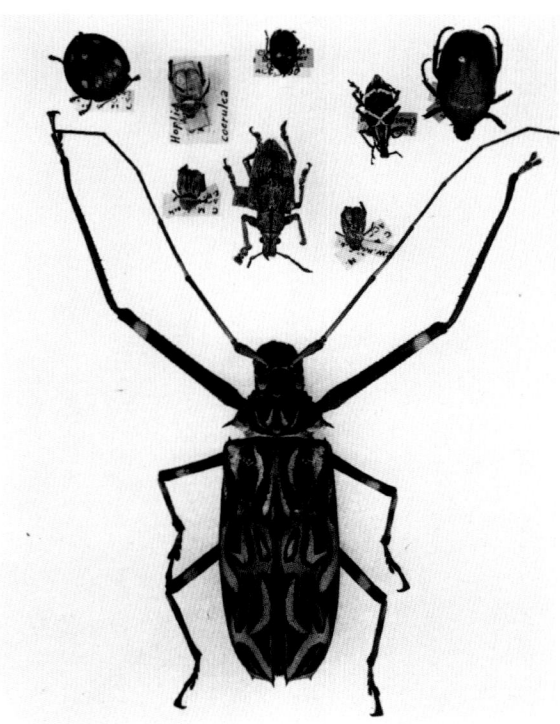

Cleveland is a city of museums, places of learning that show what we have been, what we are and what we wish to be. Their showcases and storerooms overflow with treasures—and oddities—of the natural, scientific and artistic worlds.

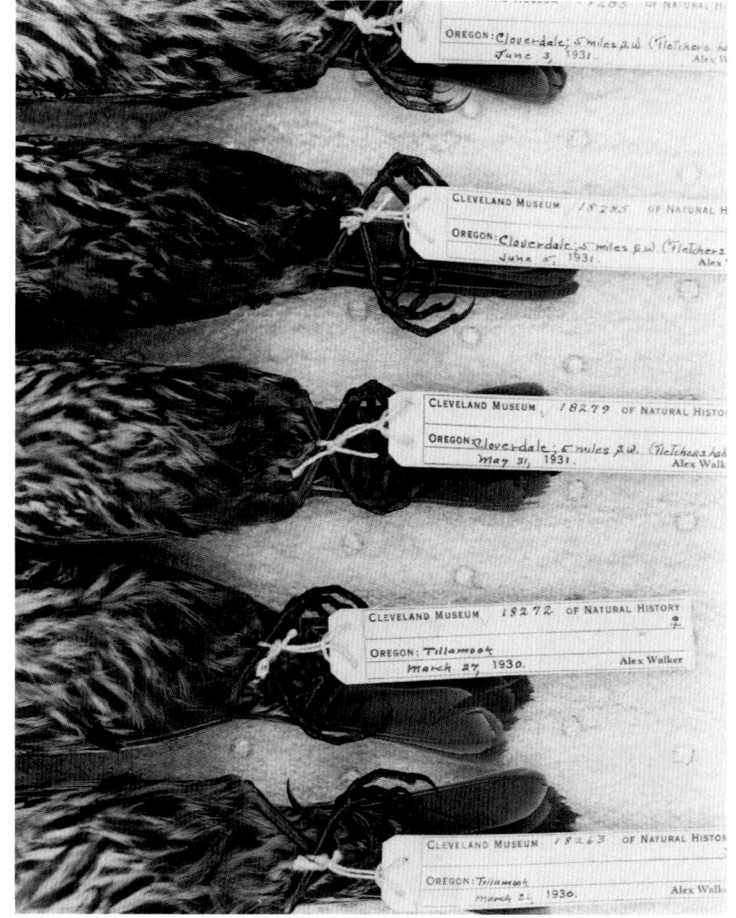

A brontosaur's bones, an Egyptian mummy, a wall of Picassos, the belly of a submarine, antique autos and Elvis's jumpsuit—they're all here: saved, preserved, studied and shared.

Halloween at the Grid: Inside has been painted outside—with a cemetery and the moon—but the mists rise from dry ice, and behind the clouds you can see faces, without masks. You can listen in on conversation, hear the bartender take orders, listen to the sound of ice against glass—the rest is theatrics.

On Halloween, we wear death's disguises, taken from folklore and low-budget movies, and find joy in acting scared.

Since 1898 the Feast of the Assumption has been a treasured summertime rite in Cleveland's Little Italy. Ask the participants.

The parish priest: "It's a high holy day observed throughout the Catholic world, first by a mass celebrating the life eternal and then by an outdoor celebration of life itself."

A restaurateur: "Everyone joins in the procession—local kids, the Knights of Columbus, politicians, policemen, Italian marching bands—everybody."

A suburban educator: "I have fond memories of going from the lemon ice at Corbo's to the pizza and sausage stands to the cavatelli dinner at the church."

A retired executive: "Last time I went it was more like the Feast of the Consumption. The trash cans were overflowing and the crowds were wall to wall."

The restaurant owner: "I'm always happy when it comes, but I'm always happy when it goes, too."

Most years they paint a green stripe down the center of Euclid Avenue for the St. Patrick's Day Parade.

Weeks or even months go by and the fading green stripe remains on the pavement, almost unnoticed. After a surprisingly long time the stripe disappears, only to reappear if everything goes according to plan the following year on the day of the parade.

Cleveland's first St. Patrick's Day Parade was held somewhere on the West Side in 1867. Several years later the parade came to downtown, where they say it has been held ever since. There, on March 17th, it always reappears. And so do those who carry some portion of the blood of the Famine Irish, the Shanty Irish, the Lace Curtain Irish and all the others who came from Ireland.

The rest of the year they go about almost unnoticed.

"The picnic. Potato salad. Hot dogs. Kool-aid in a jug. The field of long Metroparks grass. One child falls in the mud and is washed off, crying, in the creek. The horseshoes ring against the post. The volleyball net sags, and someone brings out a guitar. *If I had a hammer*, we sing, *Michael row the boat ashore*.

"The parade. Sitting on the curb watching the fire engines wheel slowly by, the convertible with the mayor of Lakewood in it. The politicians are throwing candy—we favor the one with Tootsie Rolls. Our niece is in the high school band, resplendent in white and purple and gold, the great flower of her tuba turned to the sky. We stand up and yell and wave our little flags until she turns red with embarrassment.

"Fireworks. Setting bottle rockets off in Loew Field, just after sunset. We lie on the square of our blanket as if it were a raft on a sea of grass, watching the quick arc and flash, the small comforting pop. We talk in snatches, our eyes on the sky, the small colored stars falling on us over and over again."
—Mary Grimm

Cleveland's cityscape testifies to change on a grand scale:
the rise, fall and resurgence of a two-hundred-year-old metropolis.

Juried Contributors

Dennis L. Anderson is a freelance photographer who has studied photography at Karamu House, Cuyahoga Community College and the Cleveland Photographic Society. His experience includes an internship with WVIZ-TV. A resident of Cleveland's Hough neighborhood and an employee of National City Bank, Anderson notes that the Bicentennial photography book has been a welcome personal and professional challenge.

Photographs pages 78-79
copyright ©1995 by Dennis L. Anderson

A fourth-generation Clevelander, **Herbert Ascherman** opened his photography studio in 1975. Ascherman has exhibited his personal work in Europe and Japan, published *Voyage*, a twenty-year retrospective of his black-and-white images, and displayed a dozen images in various May Shows at the Cleveland Museum of Art, where he also sponsors a purchase award. The Shaker Heights resident is an avid photography book collector and the founder and director of the Cleveland Photographic Workshop, Cleveland's only not-for-profit photography gallery.

Photographs pages 96-97 copyright ©1995 by Herbert Ascherman

Casey Batule is a bona fide product of Cleveland. He was born on Franklin Avenue and for the major part of his life has lived within three miles of the Terminal Tower. For several years he maintained a live-in studio in the Flats, virtually in the Terminal's shadow. As a former bartender, bouncer, salesman, truckdriver and laborer, Batule has met and worked with both the professional and the working classes of Cleveland. These myriad relationships inspire many of his images. Presently a resident of Lakewood, Batule is the photographer for Cleveland Metroparks and Cleveland Metroparks Zoo. He has operated a freelance commercial/industrial photography business since 1976.

Photographs pages 10, 71 and 82-83 copyright ©1995 by Casey Batule

Upon graduating from Shaker Heights High School in the summer of 1984, **Cushmere Bell** set out to become a fine art painter. His primary interest was portraiture, but when he discovered the camera in his third year at the Cleveland Institute of Art, he found it easier to relate his thoughts and ideas about people through the medium of photography and switched majors. Bell graduated in 1992, having earned an Agnes Gund Memorial Award his senior year. In the three years since his graduation, Bell's work has been exhibited throughout Cleveland, and he continues to pursue his dream of working at his art full time.

Photographs pages 65, 72-73, 111 and 142 (right) copyright ©1995 by Cushmere Bell

Stow resident **Barry J. Benjamin** has worked for the past decade as a photographer and a producer of fine art publications. He has produced the award-winning *Isles of Eden*, a large-format photography book that captures the special heritage and culture of the Bahamas' Out Islands. Benjamin's father's parents arrived in Cleveland in 1903 as immigrants from Russia during the decade immediately after the city's centenary, and he expects his daughter, Emily Marie, to celebrate the 250th anniversary of the city.

Photographs page 91 (top right, center right and bottom right) copyright ©1995 by Barry J. Benjamin

Pat Bishop has been an instructor in the bachelor of fine arts photography program at the University of Akron since 1986. Bishop's photographs focus on how gesture and expression reveal the human condition. Her images have been exhibited at the Akron Art Museum, at FAVA Gallery in Oberlin and in several May Shows at the Cleveland Museum of Art. She also has shown her work nationally. Bishop lives in Akron.

Photographs pages 24-25, 81 (top) and 141 (right) copyright ©1995 by Pat Bishop

Beachwood resident **Barbara Breen** specializes in realistic black-and-white photographs of urban landscapes and architecture taken from a back alleyway perspective that others may overlook or neglect. Breen has exhibited in solo and invitational group exhibitions at locations throughout the Midwest, including the Cleveland Museum of Art and the Cleveland Center for Contemporary Art. In addition, her work is displayed in the permanent collection of Cleveland's Society Bank. She dedicates her Bicentennial images to the memory of her father, who shared her passion for photography.

Photographs pages 32-35 and 144
copyright ©1995 by Barbara Breen

Laura Buck Balliet grew up in New York State, but moved to Cleveland in 1970 in order to attend Case Western Reserve University and the Cleveland Institute of Art. Her interest in photography began at the age of five when she begged her parents for a Kodak Brownie camera. Her shots, even then, reflected her fascination with landscape photography. Landscapes continue to be a major interest and a specialty. In addition to her creative endeavors, Balliet, who lives in Cleveland Heights, has owned and operated a medical photography business for the past twelve years.

Photographs pages 8-9, 48 (top), 101 (top left and bottom left and right) and 120-121 copyright ©1995 by Laura Buck Balliet

Linda Butler is best known for her large-format, black-and-white still-life images and interiors. Her photographs have been exhibited in museums in Canada, Japan and Italy and in more than thirty one-person shows in the United States, where her work has been widely collected by museums. Butler has published two books: *Inner Light: The Shaker Legacy* and *Rural Japan: Radiance of the Ordinary*. She and her husband moved to Ohio in 1992 and live in Gates Mills. At present, she is creating a portfolio of interiors and still-life images of Italy.

Photographs pages 40-41 and back cover (left) copyright ©1995 by Linda Butler
Photographs pages 116-117 copyright ©1995 by Linda Butler/ courtesy of the George Gund Foundation

Brian Cencula was born in September of 1969, which gave him only three months to prepare for the '70s. At age sixteen he discovered the camera and has been photographing the Cleveland area ever since. Cencula is currently doing darkroom duty on more than two years of work, largely taken between dusk and dawn because of his interest in reflected light. At the moment, he resides in an East Side suburb, where it is impossible to dine out after 10 p.m. unless your order is placed through a microphone. He plays the Lotto twice a month.

Photographs pages 46-47 copyright ©1995 by Brian Cencula

Bruce Checefsky has taken photographs for more than twenty years. His work has been featured in solo exhibits organized by HetApollohuis in the Netherlands; Artforum Galerie and Galerie Literia in Prague; the Center of Contemporary Art and Mala Galerie in Warsaw; BWA Labyrinth in Lublin, Poland; Wschodnia Galerie in Lodz, Poland; and Kastrich Galerie in Frankfurt. His images have also appeared in shows at the Museum of Modern Art in Japan and the Dia Center for the Arts in New York City. Checefsky is the recipient of grants from the Ohio Arts Council, the Foundation for Contemporary Performance Arts, the Murphy Foundation and Art Matters. He lives with his wife in the Tremont neighborhood of Cleveland.

Photographs pages 18, 100 (bottom), 113 (bottom left), 124-125, 131 (center right), title page and back cover (top) copyright ©1995 by Bruce Checefsky

William DePalma is from Lima, Ohio, and now resides in Cleveland Heights. He earned a bachelor of fine arts degree from Washington University and a master of fine arts degree in photography from Ohio University. For the past twelve years he has worked at American Greetings Corporation as a media director. DePalma has taught at Ohio University, the Maine Photographic Workshops, the University of Akron and Cuyahoga Community College. He has been awarded three separate individual artist fellowship grants from the Ohio Arts Council, along with a grant from the National Endowment for the Arts and numerous other awards.

Photographs pages 22-23 (right), 75, 81 (bottom), 85 (right), 86-87 and 131 (bottom) copyright ©1995 by William DePalma

Bill Gance grew up in Cleveland's West 65th and Lorain Avenue neighborhood, attended St. Colman's grade school and graduated from West High in 1955. Upon discharge from the U.S. Army in 1959, Gance joined the Cleveland Fire Department. He married and resided in Parma, where he and his wife, Carolyn, raised five children. After thirty years as a fireman, Gance retired in 1989. Shortly thereafter, he discovered an interest in photography. He is a member of the Cleveland Photographic Society Camera Club and is now a resident of Cinnamon Lake in Ashland County.

Photographs pages 60-61 copyright ©1995 by William V. Gance

After graduating from Case Western Reserve University, **Walter Grossman** entered military service, where he was introduced to the great Southwest. He soon fell in love with the beauty of the area and took up climbing and hiking. A camera always went along to document his travels. Early efforts produced color photographs exclusively, but gradually the Cleveland resident turned his interest to large-format, black-and-white images. Since the late 1970s, Grossman, a dentist by profession, has been represented by Wach Gallery. His photographs have been exhibited and sold in galleries across the United States, Canada and Switzerland.

Photographs pages 90-91 (left) and 94 copyright ©1995 by Walter Grossman

Joel Hauserman is a native and resident of Cleveland Heights, and makes his living as a freelance photographer. His work has appeared in galleries, collections, publications—and on refrigerators—throughout the city, the country and the world. About his Bicentennial photographs of Moses Cleaveland trees, he says: "Trees in the urban landscape are fascinating to me as beautiful forms and strong statements of survival in an often hostile environment. I found it particularly rewarding to photograph trees that are living connections to the founding of Cleveland."

Photographs pages 102-103 copyright ©1995 by Joel Hauserman

Within the last two years, artist **Masumi Hayashi** has exhibited at the Victoria and Albert Museum (England), the Rotterdam Photography Biennial (the Netherlands), the Saitama Art Museum (Japan) and the Houston Foto Fest. Her photographs have been published in *See*, *Aperture* and *Mother Jones* and are in the collections of the Victoria and Albert Museum, the Cleveland Museum of Art, the Mint Museum, the Southeast Museum of Photography, the Japanese American National Museum and the Los Angeles County Museum of Art. Hayashi has been an artist in residence at the Headlands Center for the Arts in San Francisco and the recipient of a National Endowment for the Arts Midwest fellowship grant.

"Public Square 1994," 20" x 56" panoramic photocollage, pages 20-21 copyright ©1995 by Masumi Hayashi

Jennie Jones was born in Colorado, but has lived the majority of her life in Wisconsin, Michigan and Ohio. A resident of Cleveland for seventeen years, she finds it to be a city particularly amenable to her persistent fascination with urban/industrial environments. During her time here, Cleveland has changed dramatically. Jones's work as an artist and professional photographer has been to bear witness to those changes.

Photographs pages 56-59 and 84-85 (left)
copyright ©1995 by Jennie Jones

Tina Kellogg is a senior at Cleveland State University, where she is a studio major with a focus in photography. Her photographs have been exhibited nationally and have won awards in numerous area shows. Kellogg uses photography to explore race and gender issues, including such topics as male supremacy, feminist separatism and racism and sexism within the African-American culture. A resident of Cleveland, she is currently working on a series of portraits of African-American women.

Photographs pages 26-27 and 113 (bottom right) copyright ©1995 by Ernestina Kellogg

Don Krejci received a bachelor of fine arts degree in photography in 1972 from the Cleveland Institute of Art and a master of science degree in photography in 1974 from the Illinois Institute of Technology. In 1978, he opened his own photography studio. He has exhibited widely, and his architectural photography has been featured in *Metropolitan Home* magazine. Krejci is a native Clevelander who resides in Orange Village with his wife and daughter.

Photographs pages 118-119 and 143
copyright ©1995 by Donald Krejci

Daniel Levin specializes in photographing people on location for corporate and editorial clients, including IBM, Ameritech, Caterpillar, MBNA, United Airlines, *Forbes* and *Business Week*. Documenting people who work on the water is the subject that most interests him personally. He recently spent four days under the Atlantic on the U.S. Navy's newest fast-attack nuclear submarine, photographing the sailors aboard. Levin graduated with honors from the Rochester Institute of Technology. He and his wife, Nancy, live in Shaker Heights with their two daughters.

Photographs pages 52-55 copyright ©1995 by Daniel Levin

Helen Liggett lives in Cleveland Heights and works at Cleveland State University as an associate professor of urban studies. She is coeditor of *Spatial Practices*, and her scholarly work on the production of conceptual tools in the intersection between cultural politics and public policy has appeared in *Planning Theory*, *Intersight*, *Urban Affairs Quarterly* and the *Minnesota Review*. Liggett's Bicentennial images of Cleveland's West Side Market represent a conviction, developed in their making, of the inestimable contribution that public spaces make to urban vitality.

Photographs pages 42-43
copyright ©1995 by Helen Liggett

Medina native **Ron Linek** is the staff photographer for Baldwin-Wallace College. His assignments have taken him from everyday college events to the rain forests of Ecuador and flood-damaged towns along the Mississippi. An avid traveler, Linek has a particular interest in the diverse cultures and folk art of Latin America. A recent study trip found him photographing economic development in Nicaragua. As a former photojournalist for the Sun Newspapers and Medina County *Gazette*, Linek won numerous awards from the Ohio News Photographers Association. He has also lived in Spain, photographing the country and teaching English with his wife.

Photographs pages 88-89 and 92-93 copyright ©1995 by Ron Linek

Michael Loderstedt received a bachelor of fine arts degree in printmaking from East Carolina University in 1982 and a master of fine arts degree in multimedia from Kent State University in 1985. His major exhibitions include "Ohio Selections" at the Cleveland Center for Contemporary Art (1990) and the "Invitational" at the Cleveland Museum of Art (1991). Loderstedt has had four solo shows at Cleveland's William Busta Gallery and has exhibited in New York, Pittsburgh, Santa Monica, Japan and Canada. He lives in Cleveland, less than a block from Lake Erie, the subject of some of his Bicentennial imagery.

Photographs pages 50-51, 101 (top right and center right), 111 (top) and 131 (top and center left) copyright ©1995 by Michael Loderstedt

Roger Mastroianni is a self-taught freelance photographer who has worked in the Midwest for nearly fifteen years. He started his career shooting professional sports for United Press International and stage productions for the Cleveland Play House. Currently his corporate clients include many Fortune 500 companies. He is also a regular contributor to *Business Week*, *Forbes*, *Fortune*, *Newsweek*, the *New York Times* and *Rolling Stone*. Mastroianni shoots for most of Cleveland's theater companies, as well as the Cleveland Orchestra. He lives in South Euclid with his wife, Barbara, and their two sons.

Photographs pages 22 (top left and bottom left) and 62-63
copyright ©1995 by Roger Mastroianni

James M. McCarthy grew up in Berea and discovered photography as a teenager in the late 1960s. Through it he began to explore his relationships to family and friends, nature and, more recently, social issues. The camera has helped him earn a living as a journalist. Whether photographing volunteers serving their neighbors on Cleveland's near West Side—the subject of his Bicentennial imagery—Cambodian refugees finding a new life in New Hampshire or the struggling farmers and fishermen of Maine, where he now lives, McCarthy seeks to affirm our common humanity and interdependence in a world of finite resources.

Photographs pages 104-105 (bottom left and right), 106-107, 112 and 113 (top) copyright ©1995 by James M. McCarthy

Native Clevelander **Nancy McEntee** grew up and currently resides on the city's West Side. She received her bachelor of fine arts degree in photography from the Cleveland Institute of Art in 1984 and her master of fine arts degree from Bard College. She is presently an assistant professor of photography at the Institute of Art. Her interest in Cleveland's Irish-American community stems from a long-running documentation of her own family, whose ancestors were originally from County Mayo. McEntee exhibits her work nationally and is a 1995 recipient of an Ohio Arts Council individual artist fellowship grant.

Photographs pages 114-115 and 128-129 copyright ©1995 by Nancy M. McEntee

Judith McMillan grew up in Cleveland and has spent most of her life here. Once her children were in school, she returned to school herself and graduated from the Cleveland Institute of Art in 1990. An avid gardener and naturalist, she now finds her time divided between her orchids and gardens, her family and dog, and her photography. McMillan uses the camera to explore the natural world. Her work has been exhibited in the May Show at the Cleveland Museum of Art and is in public and private collections.

Photocollage pages 108-109 and photographs pages 122-123 copyright ©1995 by Judith K. McMillan

Robert Muller's interest in photography was initiated by his father's love of travel. They started traveling together on Sunday drives to Cleveland's Flats and later, over a three-year period, made a series of trips through Europe. These experiences provided Muller with his first body of published work. In 1987 he received a bachelor of fine arts degree in painting from the Cleveland Institute of Art, and he currently works in the Institute's foundation department. Since 1981 he has operated a commercial photography business based in University Circle. In 1994 Muller received an Ohio Arts Council individual artist fellowship grant for his photographs of the Cuyahoga River, some of which are published here.

Photographs pages 11-14 copyright ©1995 by Robert Muller

Renee Psiakis was born and raised in Cleveland. She has lived in every part of the city and now resides in Cleveland Heights. She is married to photographer William DePalma and has a daughter, Anna, who is the subject of many of her photographs. Psiakis attended Ohio University both as an undergraduate and then as a graduate student, receiving her master of fine arts degree in photography. She is currently teaching at the University of Akron and at the Maine Photographic Workshops. Psiakis has been the recipient of three separate individual artist fellowship grants from the Ohio Arts Council.

Photographs pages 76-77 copyright ©1995 by Renee Psiakis

Lakewood resident **Mark Quintero** is a former U.S. Army photographer who was awarded the Commendation Medal, the Fourth Estate Award and two Keith L. Ware Awards (the Army's equivalent of the Pulitzer Prize). After leaving the service, Quintero was retained by the West German government to teach photography at Panzer Kaserne. He has also worked in the photography department of NASA Lewis Research Center in Cleveland and as chief photographer for Fort Devens, Massachusetts. He currently prints Cibachrome photos at Chromatech in Independence.

Cover photograph and photographs page 15 copyright ©1995 by Mark R. Quintero

John Rechin, a native of Ohio, began his love affair with the art of photography in 1987. Since that time he has earned a bachelor of fine arts degree from the Savannah College of Art and Design, exhibited his images in both Georgia and Ohio, and worked as a staff photographer for the *Georgia Guardian* and as an editorial photographer for *Sights and Sounds of Savannah Jazz*. Rechin currently resides in Waite Hill, freelances in photography and is employed by the Western Reserve Historical Society.

Photographs pages 6-7, 48 (bottom), 100 (top) and 130 copyright ©1995 by John G. Rechin

Emily S. Rosen was born in Cleveland and presently resides in Cleveland Heights. She earned a master of fine arts degree from the Rochester Institute of Technology in 1984 and enjoys photography, cycling and the outdoors. For her Bicentennial project, Rosen biked from Public Square in downtown Cleveland to Public Square in downtown Willoughby Hills. She covered the 18.6-mile stretch at an average speed of 12.8 mph and took pleasure in photographing the interesting, beautiful or curious sights that her unhurried pace and ground-level perspective allowed her to see.

Photographs pages 36-39 copyright ©1995 by Emily S. Rosen

Clevelander **Idris Salih** is a 1995 graduate of Ohio University. At age five, he wanted to be an artist like his father. But at the age of ten, he was drawn to the world of science, especially the study of light and chemistry. When he was introduced to photography, it was love at first sight. Now Salih looks forward to uniting the two loves of his childhood in a career as a fashion photographer.

Photographs pages 44-45 and 80
copyright ©1995 by Idris Salih

Yvonne R. Sanderson is a native Clevelander who now resides in South Euclid. A licensed pilot, she owns Focal Plane Photography, which specializes in aerial photography. Sanderson is a graduate of the International Center of Photography and serves as the executive director of a suburban chamber of commerce. Her photographs are in the collection of Cleveland's Progressive Corporation.

Endpapers (front and back) and photograph pages 134-135
copyright ©1995 by Yvonne R. Sanderson

Richard Sanna and **Heidi Staudt-Sanna** were born in the mid-1960s, he in Brooklyn, New York, and she in Richmond Heights, Ohio. Their paths did not converge until 1986, when they met while each was working toward a bachelor of fine arts degree in photography at the School of Visual Arts in New York City. After graduation, they moved to Ohio, settled in Painesville and were married in 1991. In their spare time they enjoy making art and gardening, but their favorite hobby is spending time with each other, their dogs—Cairo, Wegman and Zena—and their cat, Gus.

Photographs pages 66-67 copyright ©1995 by Richard Sanna and Heidi Staudt-Sanna

Cleveland-born photographer **Jean Schnell** specializes in black-and-white portraiture. The Cleveland Heights resident attempts to convey the idiosyncratic nature of each individual she photographs. Schnell's work has been featured nationally in advertising campaigns, magazines and galleries, and she has recently signed with a New York stock agency.

Photographs pages 126-127
copyright ©1995 by Jean Schnell

Thomas Simon has worked as a freelance photographer and writer since 1976. His work has appeared in regional and national newspapers and magazines, as well as various foreign publications. His specialties include business portraits, industrial photography, reportage and documentation. After finishing an undergraduate degree in anthropology, Simon moved to the West Coast, where he worked for a time as a longshoreman, among other jobs. Returning to Ohio, he realized that Cleveland was home after hearing Richard Strauss's *Also Sprach Zarathustra* played on the accordion at a picnic.

Photographs pages 64 (top and center), 70, 104 (top left) and back cover (right)
copyright ©1995 by Thomas Simon

Don Snyder was born in Brooklyn, New York, and graduated from Colgate University in 1970 and Cleveland's Cooper School of Art in 1975. After assisting various photographers for several years, in 1983 he opened his own studio, specializing in corporate portraiture and annual reports. In addition, Snyder serves on the boards of Cleveland Works and the Goodrich Gannett Neighborhood Center and provides photography for these organizations. He was a founding member of the Ohio Northcoast chapter of the American Society of Media Photographers (ASMP) and served as its president for two years.

Photographs pages 28-31 and back cover (bottom) copyright ©1995 by Don Snyder

Barney Taxel grew up in New York City. He came to Cleveland in 1967 to study architecture at Case Western Reserve University, but eventually changed his concentration to creative photography. A student of Nicholas Hlobeczy and Minor White, Taxel is a commercial photographer whose specialties are food, product, image transfer, architectural and corporate photography. He has exhibited extensively since 1971 and has received numerous awards for his personal and commercial art. Taxel lives in Cleveland Heights with his wife, writer Laura Taxel, and their three sons.

Photographs pages 16-17 and 132-133
copyright ©1995 by Barney Taxel

David M. Thum grew up on Cleveland's East Side. He graduated in 1977 from the Rochester Institute of Technology with a degree in professional photography. From 1977 to 1984 Thum was the chief photographic archivist at the Cuyahoga County Archives, where he created a collection of Cleveland images drawn from his original photography and photographic copies made from historic paintings and photographs. His work has been featured in a number of northern Ohio galleries and publications. Now living on Cleveland's West Side, he divides his time between teaching, maintaining his architectural photography business, photographing works of fine art for publication and exhibiting his images.

Photographs pages 95 and 98-99 copyright ©1995 by David M. Thum

Willoughby Hills resident **Stephen Travarca** graduated from the Cooper School of Art in Cleveland in 1977 and has worked as a medical photographer at the Cleveland Clinic Foundation since 1978. His interests also include portraiture, commercial and fine art photography and, most recently, electronic imaging. Travarca's work has been exhibited in the Willoughby Fine Arts Juried Exhibition in 1993 and 1994.

Photograph page 19
copyright ©1995 by Stephen A. Travarca

Peter Wach, a native Clevelander, is an international fine art photography dealer. As owner and director of Wach Gallery in Avon Lake, he has exhibited the masterworks of nineteenth- and twentieth-century photographers throughout the United States and Europe. Wach served on the board of directors of the Association of International Photography Dealers (AIPAD) during the 150th anniversary year of photography. He is currently president of the Northeast Ohio Art Dealers Association (NOADA). His work as a photographer reflects a commitment to Cleveland and the art and history of photography.

Photographs pages 68-69
copyright ©1995 by Peter M. Wach

"Community Shoot" Contributors

Deborah Anzick
Photograph page 142 (left) copyright ©1995 by Deborah Anzick

Janet Century
Photograph page 74 copyright ©1995 by Janet Century

Marius Chira
Photograph pages 48-49 (right) copyright ©1995 by Marius Chira

Michael Edwards
Photograph on copyright page copyright ©1995 by Michael Edwards

Adam Misztal
Photograph page 110 copyright ©1995 by Adam Misztal

Robert H. Wetzler
Photographs pages 64 (bottom) and 65 (bottom)
copyright ©1995 by Robert H. Wetzler

Photographers' Exhibition Images
(Alphabetical order)

Dennis L. Anderson 78-79 (center)
Deborah Anzick 142 (left)
Herbert Ascherman 96
Laura Buck Balliet 8
Casey Batule 82-83
Cushmere Bell 65 (top)
Barry J. Benjamin 91 (top right)
Pat Bishop 81 (top)
Barbara Breen 34
Linda Butler 41 (top)
Brian Cencula 46 (top)
Janet Century 74
Bruce Checefsky 125 (bottom right)
Marius Chira 48-49 (right)
William DePalma 85 (right)
Michael Edwards Copyright page
Bill Gance 61
Walter Grossman 90-91 (left)
Joel Hauserman 103 (right)
Masumi Hayashi 20-21
Jennie Jones 56-57 (center)
Tina Kellogg 26 (top)
Don Krejci 118
Daniel Levin 52-53 (bottom left)
Helen Liggett 43 (top right)
Ron Linek 88-89
Michael Loderstedt 50-51
Roger Mastroianni 62
James M. McCarthy 106 (top)
Nancy McEntee 129
Judith McMillan 108-109
Adam Misztal 110
Robert Muller 12 (top right)
Renee Psiakis 76 (bottom left)
Mark Quintero 15 (bottom)
John Rechin 130
Emily S. Rosen 38 (top)
Idris Salih 44 (top left)
Yvonne R. Sanderson Endpaper (front)
Richard Sanna and Heidi Staudt-Sanna 67 (bottom left)
Jean Schnell 126-127 (top center)
Thomas Simon 70 (top)
Don Snyder 31 (top right)
Barney Taxel 132-133
David M. Thum 98 (bottom)
Stephen Travarca 19
Peter Wach 68 (right)
Robert H. Wetzler 64 (bottom)

The images listed above were exhibited at the Cleveland Center for Contemporary Art from October 13 through November 11, 1995. The exhibition was made possible by the generous support of KSK Color Lab Inc., makers of custom prints of selected color images in the show, and by The Bonfoey Company and Morse Graphic Art Supply Company, providers of matting and framing.

Index

Photographers' Work
(Numerical order)

Cover Mark Quintero
Endpapers (front and back)
    Yvonne R. Sanderson
Title page Bruce Checefsky
Copyright page Michael Edwards
6-7 John Rechin
8-9 Laura Buck Balliet
10 Casey Batule
11-14 Robert Muller
16-17 Barney Taxel
18 Bruce Checefsky
19 Stephen Travarca
20-21 Masumi Hayashi
22 (top left and bottom left)
    Roger Mastroianni
22-23 (right) William DePalma
24-25 Pat Bishop
26-27 Tina Kellogg
28-31 Don Snyder
32-35 Barbara Breen
36-39 Emily S. Rosen
40-41 Linda Butler
42-43 Helen Liggett
44-45 Idris Salih
46-47 Brian Cencula
48 (top) Laura Buck Balliet;
    (bottom) John Rechin
48-49 (right) Marius Chira
50-51 Michael Loderstedt
52-55 Daniel Levin
56-59 Jennie Jones
60-61 Bill Gance
62-63 Roger Mastroianni
64 (top and center)
    Thomas Simon; (bottom)
    Robert H. Wetzler
65 (top) Cushmere Bell;
    (bottom) Robert H. Wetzler
66-67 Richard Sanna and
    Heidi Staudt-Sanna
68-69 Peter Wach
70 Thomas Simon
71 Casey Batule
72-73 Cushmere Bell
74 Janet Century
75 William DePalma
76-77 Renee Psiakis
78-79 Dennis L. Anderson
80 Idris Salih
81 (top) Pat Bishop; (bottom)
    William DePalma
82-83 Casey Batule
84-85 (left) Jennie Jones

85 (right) William DePalma
86-87 William DePalma
88-89 Ron Linek
90-91 (left) Walter Grossman
91 (top right, center right and
    bottom right) Barry J. Benjamin
92-93 Ron Linek
94 Walter Grossman
95 David M. Thum
96-97 Herbert Ascherman
98-99 David M. Thum
100 (top) John Rechin; (bottom)
    Bruce Checefsky
101 (top left and bottom left
    and right) Laura Buck Balliet;
    (top right and center right)
    Michael Loderstedt
102-103 Joel Hauserman
104 (top left) Thomas Simon;
    (bottom left) James M.
    McCarthy
104-105 (right) James M. McCarthy
106-107 James M. McCarthy
108-109 Judith McMillan
110 Adam Misztal
111 (top) Michael Loderstedt;
    (bottom) Cushmere Bell
112 James M. McCarthy
113 (top) James M. McCarthy;
    (bottom left) Bruce Checefsky;
    (bottom right) Tina Kellogg
114-115 Nancy McEntee
116-117 Linda Butler
118-119 Don Krejci
120-121 Laura Buck Balliet
122-123 Judith McMillan
124-125 Bruce Checefsky
126-127 Jean Schnell
128-129 Nancy McEntee
130 John Rechin
131 (top and center left)
    Michael Loderstedt;
    (center right) Bruce Checefsky;
    (bottom) William DePalma
132-133 Barney Taxel
134-135 Yvonne R. Sanderson
141 (right) Pat Bishop
142 (left) Deborah Anzick;
    (right) Cushmere Bell
143 Don Krejci
144 Barbara Breen
Back cover (top) Bruce Checefsky;
    (left) Linda Butler;
    (bottom) Don Snyder;
    (right) Thomas Simon

Writers' Credits
(Numerical order)

6-7 Dick Feagler
8-15 William R. Johnson
16-17 Laura Taxel
18 (left) Mary Grimm
20-21 Jeff Hagan
22-23 Roberta Hubbard Lubetkin
24-25 Derek VanPelt
26-27 Claudia Rankine
28-31 Michael Dreyfuss
32-35 Les Roberts
36-39 Dan Chaon
40-41 Richard Hawley
42-43 David Patterson
44-45 Jordan Lubetkin
46-47 Brian Cencula
48-49 Diana Tittle
50-51 David Beach
52-53 John Tidyman
54-55 Diana Tittle
56-59 Carol Poh Miller
60-61 Peter Jedick
62-63 Mark Gottlieb
64-65 Buster Jackson
66-67 Eric Broder
68-69 Derek VanPelt
70-71 Michael Heaton
72-75 Sheila Schwartz
76-77 Charles Oberndorf
78-79 Roberta Hubbard Lubetkin
80-81 Mark Gottlieb
84-85 Eric Broder
86-87 Mark Winegardner
88-89 Diana Tittle
90-91 Mark Gottlieb
92-93 Rice Hershey
94-95 Wilma Salisbury
98-99 Wilma Salisbury
100-101 Claudia Rankine
102-103 David Beach
104-107 Dennis Dooley
108-109 Gary Engle
110-111 Diana Tittle
112-113 Richard Hawley
114-115 Edward J. Walsh
116-117 Linda Butler
118-121 Bill Rudman
122-123 David Patterson
124-125 Charles Oberndorf
126-127 Rice Hershey
128-129 Edward J. Walsh
130-131 Mary Grimm
132-133 Laura Taxel

Location of Photographs
(Numerical order)

All locations are in the City of Cleveland unless otherwise noted.

Cover Lakewood
Endpaper (front) Canterbury Golf Club, Shaker Heights
Title page Tremont
Copyright page West Side
6-7 View of Cleveland from Wildwood Park jetty, Euclid
8 South Chagrin Reservation, Cleveland Metroparks
9 Euclid Creek Reservation, Cleveland Metroparks
10 Brecksville Reservation, Cleveland Metroparks
11 Burton Township, Geauga County
12 (top left) Russell Park, Portage County; (top right) North of Kent, Ohio, near the Botzum Waste Water Treatment Plant; (center left and bottom right) Gorge Metro Park, Akron; (bottom left) Kent
13 Gorge Metro Park, Akron
14 (top left) Cuyahoga Valley National Recreation Area; (top right and bottom) The Flats
15 (top) Ontario Stone Corporation, Whiskey Island; (bottom) Columbus Road, The Flats
16-17 The Osterland Company
18 Tremont
19 Huron Road and West 3rd Street
20-21 Public Square
22 (top left and bottom left) Meridia Hillcrest Hospital, Mayfield Heights
22-23 (right) Cleveland Heights
24 Great Northern Mall, North Olmsted
25 (top and bottom) Great Northern Mall, North Olmsted; (center) Kenneth's, Beachwood
28-31 Kirkland neighborhood near East 40th Street and Superior Avenue
32-35 Track Road, near E. 55th Street and Broadway
36-37 Euclid Avenue, East Cleveland
38-39 Euclid Avenue from Euclid to Willoughby
40 (top) Belgian Village; (left) Chestnut Hills; (bottom right) Orange Village, Cuyahoga County
41 (top) Cleveland Heights; (bottom) Orange Village, Cuyahoga County
42-43 West Side Market
44-45 Coventry Village, Cleveland Heights
46 (top) Little Italy; (center left) Cleveland Heights; (bottom left) Wickliffe; (bottom right) Cleveland
47 (top) Beachwood (bottom) Shaker Heights
48 (top left) Rockefeller Park; (bottom left) North Chagrin Reservation, Cleveland Metroparks
48-49 (right) Wade Lagoon
50-51 View of Lake Erie from E. 152nd Street, South Euclid
52-53 Lake Erie: (top left) Cleveland Department of Public Utilities Water Division; (top center) Ohio Department of Natural Resources Water Division; (second from right and bottom center) Cleveland Fire Department; (top right and bottom right) United States Coast Guard
54-55 Port of Cleveland
56-59 C&P Ore Dock, Whiskey Island
62-63 LTV Steel Company
64-65 Downtown Cleveland
66-67 Lorain Avenue; (bottom left) State Street, Painesville
68-69 Rock and Roll Hall of Fame and Museum
70 Savoy Restaurant (defunct), Prospect Avenue
71 Major Hoopple's, The Flats
72-73 (left) 6 Street Under
73 (right) Elks Club
74 Cedar Point, Sandusky
75 Headlands State Park, Mentor
76-77 Cuyahoga County Fair, Berea
78 (left) Hough
78-79 (center) E. 55th Street and Woodland Avenue
79 (right) League Park
80 Cedar Road
81 (top) Foster Pool, Lakewood Park, Lakewood; (bottom) Jefferson Park
82-83 Valley Parkway, Cleveland Metroparks
84-85 (left) Shooters, The Flats
85 (right) West Side
86-87 Jacobs Field
88-89 La Iglesia Cristiana, Inc., Lorain Avenue
90-91 (left) The Temple-Tifereth Israel, University Circle
91 (top right, center right and bottom right) Gates Mills
92-93 The Islamic Center of Cleveland, Parma
94 St. Michael Church, Tremont
95 St. John's Episcopal Church-Historic, Ohio City
96 St. Elias Church, Brooklyn
97 (top row, from left) St. Elizabeth's Church, Buckeye Road; St. John AME Church, E. 40th Street; St. Peters Church, E. 17th Street; (second row, from left) Pilgrim Congregational Church, Tremont; St. Maron Church, Carnegie Avenue; St. Malachi's Church, Washington Avenue; (third row, from left) Fairmount Presbyterian Church, Cleveland Heights; Cathedral of St. John The Evangelist, Superior Avenue; St. Luke's Episcopal Church, West 78th Street; (bottom row, from left) Chabad House of Cleveland, University Heights; Freedom Christian Church, East Cleveland; St. Patrick's Church, Ohio City
98 (top) St. Adalbert Church, Adalbert Street; (center left) St. Stephen's Church, W. 54th Street; (center right) Trinity Cathedral, E. 22nd Street; (bottom) St. Vitas Church, Glass Avenue
99 St. Patrick's Church, Ohio City
100 (top) Kirtland Temple Reorganized Church of Jesus Christ of Latter Day Saints, Kirtland; (bottom) Scranton Cemetery, Tremont
101 (top left and bottom left and right) Erie Street Cemetery; (top right and center right) Lake View Cemetery
102-103 (left) "Moses Cleaveland" white oak, Lutheran Cemetery
103 (right) "Moses Cleaveland" red oak, Turney Road, Garfield Heights
104-105 St. Herman's House of Hospitality, Franklin Boulevard
106-107 St. Patrick's Church, Ohio City
108-109 E. 120th Street and Miles Avenue community garden; Hampshire Road community garden, Cleveland Heights; Central neighborhood community garden
111 (top) South Euclid; (bottom) The Factory, Cleveland Institute of Art, University Circle
112 Calvary Reformed Church of America, W. 65th Street
113 (top) Calvary Reformed Church of America, W. 65th Street; (bottom left) Tremont; (bottom right) St. Adalbert School, E. 83rd Street
116-117 Severance Hall, University Circle
120-121 The Flats
122 (top left) Allen Memorial Medical Library, University Circle; (top right and bottom left) Cleveland Museum of Natural History, University Circle
122-123 (bottom center) Cleveland Museum of Art, University Circle
123 (top left and bottom right) Cleveland Museum of Natural History, University Circle; (top right and bottom left) Western Reserve Historical Society, University Circle
124-125 The Grid, W. 9th Street
126-127 Little Italy
128 (top left) St. Colman's Church, W. 65th Street; (bottom left, top right, center right and bottom right) Downtown Cleveland
129 Edgewater Park
130 Gates Mills
131 (top and center left) South Euclid; (center right) Tremont; (bottom) Cleveland Heights
132-133 North Coast Harbor
134-135 Aerial view of Cleveland
141 (right) Cleveland Center for Contemporary Art
142 (left) Lorain Avenue; (right) E. 4th Street
143 Chagrin Valley Hunt Club, Gates Mills
144 Broadway neighborhood
Endpaper (back) Edgewater Park

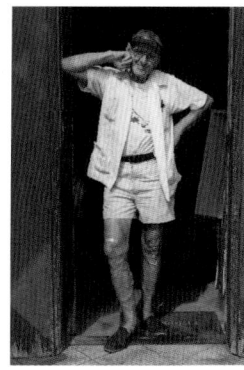

Acknowledgments

The Cleveland Bicentennial Commission thanks the following individuals and companies whose generous support and assistance helped to make possible both this book and the related exhibition of selected images at the Cleveland Center for Contemporary Art.

Corporate Cosponsors
(Level of In-kind Contribution)

Emerson Press
Morse Graphic Art
 Supply Company
$10,000 and above

Alling and Cory
American Greetings Corporation
The Bonfoey Company
Forest City Bookbindery (a division of the Chilcote Company)
KSK Color Lab Inc.
S. D. Warren Company
$5,000

Dodd Camera & Video
KD Color Lab
Midtown Imaging
TSI Typesetting Service Inc.
$2,500

Editorial Advisory Committee
Carolyn Bradley
Henry Eaton
Mary Grimm
Kei McMillin
Robert Palmer
Carol Rivchun
Sam Thomas III

Book and Exhibition Jury*
Susan Channing
Toby Lewis
Mark Schwartz
Toni Starinsky**
Dr. Evan H. Turner

*selected the photographers asked to contribute to "Images from the Heart" and decided which of the published photographs should be exhibited
**member only of the book jury

Contributing Writers
David Beach
Eric Broder
Linda Butler
Brian Cencula
Dan Chaon
Dennis Dooley
Michael Dreyfuss
Gary Engle
Dick Feagler
Mark Gottlieb
Mary Grimm
Jeff Hagan
Richard Hawley
Michael Heaton
Rice Hershey
Buster Jackson
Peter Jedick
William R. Johnson
Jordan Lubetkin
Roberta Hubbard Lubetkin
Carol Poh Miller
Charles Oberndorf
David Patterson
Claudia Rankine
Les Roberts
Bill Rudman
Wilma Salisbury
Sheila Schwartz
Laura Taxel
John Tidyman
Diana Tittle
Derek VanPelt
Edward J. Walsh
Mark Winegardner

Volunteers
Gary Engle (Editing)
Mary Koster (Project coordination)
Nancy Levin (Archive)

Friends and Advisors
Ken Alvey
Brigid Andrews
ASM International
John T. Bailey
John Barcza
Dennis Barrie
Maida Barron
Agnes Batule
Father Bob Begin
Mary Ann Bienerth
Ed Bily
James A. Birch
John Blazek
Dewey Brannon
Brass Ring Photography/ Gerald Penca
Denis Breno
Penny Buchanan
Robert Calmer
Laurence Channing
David Chilcote
Julias Ciaccia
Gary Clark
Cleveland Browns
Cleveland Fire Department Second Battalion
Cleveland Indians
Cleveland's Irish-American community
Rosalie Cohen
Dan Craven
Nancy Cronin
Iman Fawaz Damra
Rick Dimitrov
Father Tony Dodd
Dennis Dooley
Oliver F. Emerson
Mort Epstein
Karen and Tom Esper
Michele Felger
Karen Ferguson
Donald J. Fox
Michele Fuller
G & R Advertising
The Reverend Armando Contreras Galarza
Kenneth Gazdag, Sr.
Susie Gharrity
Glenville Development Center
Stanley Gordon
Marty Goren
Regina Gorie
John Grabowski
David Gray
Ralph E. Green
Richard Greiner, Jr.
Amy Gressell
Elvera Gruttadauria
Marcia G. Hall
Dyane Hanslik
Eric Harris
Teresa Hauck
Heck's Catering Service
Tom Hinson
Meecham and Robin Hitchcock
Hough Area Partners in Progress
Hough Norwood Family Health Centers
Charles Hurlbut
Brian Huth
Valerie Johnson
Jennie Jones
Staci Jones
Marilyn Jontzen
Susan Kandzer
Cathryn Kapp
Karamu House
Deborah A. Kavulich
Koby Photo Supply
Dan Kochevar
Rob Kochis
Dean Kock
Jeff Konishi
Joel Koslen
Ben Kotowski
Ed Kubasky
LTV Steel Company
League Park
Kathryn Lee
David London
Robert Lyons
Heather Mackey
Lawrence and Nancy Malm
David Margiotta
Victor Martinez
Robert Mayer
Nancy McCann
Michele McCombs
Joseph W. McEntee
Colleen McQuaid
Randy McShepard
Olga M. Merela
Metro Helicopter Inc.
Jeff Mieyal
Betsy Molnar
Richard Moore
Meg Morilak
Ruth Morrison
Bill Nagode
National City Bank/NCC
Dean Noonan
Northeast Ohio Art Dealers Association
Father David Novak
Ohio & Western Pennsylvania Dock Company employees
Karen Opalek
Rabbi Michael Oppenheimer
Pat Papash
Mark Pastor
Jeff Pavic
Jennifer Pickering
Kermit Pike
Ruth Popovich
Tom Punchak
Bill Ragg
Randy Rowley
Bill Rudman
Kathy Ruggeri
Dennis Sadowski
Fran Saltzman
Mark Sanderson
Gary Sangster
W. D. Sharp
Kishore Shaw
Sister Madeline Shemo
Rick Sherlock
Nancy Shimp
Karen Skunta
Sandra Slaughter
Janus Small
George Smith
Don Snyder
Katherine Solender
Gene Stermole
Stouffer's Renaissance Cleveland Hotel
Dan and Kathy Struna
John Szilagyi
Barney and Laura Taxel
Rosalind V. Taylor
Mark R. Tomasch
Trans-Media Productions, Inc.
Bill Trausch
William Turoczy
Peter Wach
Jonathan Wayne
Dann Witczak
Robert Woide
Richard Yuhas
Kim Zarney
Ann Zoller

Cleveland Bicentennial Commission
Robert W. Gillespie
Richard W. Pogue
Co-chairs

Margot James Copeland
Alan S. Kopit
Vice-chairs

Richard D. Acton
Judge Ronald B. Adrine
James M. Biggar
Rena J. Blumberg
Edward B. Brandon
William E. Butler
Henry F. Eaton
Richard L. Ehrlich
Wayne Embry
Allen H. Ford
Joseph T. Gorman
Carole F. Hoover
Alex Machaskee
Darlene Evans McCoy
Dr. Howard A. Mims
Lindsay J. Morganthaler
Thomas W. Morris
The Reverend Allison F. Phillips
Bishop Anthony M. Pilla
Clara T. Rankin
Albert B. Ratner
Jerry Sue Thornton, Ph.D.
Joseph A. Valencic
Judge Jose A. Villanueva
Martin D. Walker

David T. Abbott
Executive Director